Earth Works

Davey R. Hago

Earth Works

Readings
for
Backyard
Gardeners

Nancy R. Hugo

University Press of Virginia

Charlottesville and London

Clare Leighton's wood-engravings are reproduced from *Four Hedges: A Gardener's Chronicle* (New York: Macmillan), 1935, with the kind permission of David Roland Leighton.

Earlier versions or portions of many of these essays originally appeared in the Hanover County, Va., *Herald-Progress, Horticulture, Fine Gardening*, the Richmond *Times-Dispatch, Virginia Wildlife*, and *Garden Club of Virginia Journal*.

The University Press of Virginia
Printed in the United States of America

First published 1997

⊗ The paper used in this publication meets the miniumum requirements of the American National Standard for Information Sciences—Permanence of Paper for Printed Library Materials, ANSI Z39.48-1984.

Library of Congress Cataloging-in-Publication Data

Hugo, Nancy R.
      Earth works : readings for backyard gardeners / Nancy R. Hugo.
      p.   cm.
      Includes bibliographical references (p.   ).
      ISBN 0-8139-1754-9 (cloth : alk. paper)
      2. Gardening—Virginia.   I. Title.
   SB453.2.V5H84   1997
   635.9'09755—dc21   97-10374
                                                                      CIP

FOR MY MOTHER

Contents

Contents

May

June

July

August

Contents

Illustrations

All illustrations are reproduced from wood engravings by Clare Leighton, published in *Four Hedges: A Gardener's Chronicle* (Macmillan, 1935), except for the illustration for December.

Preface

This collection includes descriptions of some of my favorite plants, tools, techniques, and gardening experiences. Many of the essays appear almost as they were originally published, others have been rewritten, and some are new, but I hope they all communicate something timeless about the gardening process.

Some essays were easy to revise in a way that allowed me to include information I've learned since they were first written, but two of the older essays resisted revision so resolutely I would like to include postscripts to them here. I could not, for example, add to an essay that described dreaming about growing cyclamen new information about how my cyclamen planting turned out. I would like you to know, however, that cyclamen now spill down the bank under my oak just as I dreamed they would in "Cyclamen Flourish in January Dreams." I've even discovered the plants will seed-in—an unexpected bonus garden writer Elizabeth Lawrence hadn't prepared me for, but I should warn you that squirrels like to dig up young cyclamen tubers.

The other outcome I would like to report relates to vertical mulching. At the end of "Arboreal Acupuncture Helps Trees

Survive" my husband John and I were about to drill holes in our compacted heavy clay soil to try to mitigate the damage done by heavy equipment. Not only did the holes John drilled and I filled with pea gravel keep our trees alive, but I'm convinced those breathing holes improved the health of soil in the entire area we "drilled." Beware of straining your back if you're trying to use such a heavy-duty augur, however; I can still see the terrific wrench it administered to John's body every time the augur hit something it couldn't penetrate.

And a note about two things that might be confusing. Contrary to what the order of these essays might imply, my daughter was a child before she was an adult. In an April essay I refer to her as a grown-up gardener, in a September essay as a teenager, and in a November essay as a child again. No, Kate is not a time traveler. The essays are organized according to the month in which they appeared or for which they would be appropriate, but they are clearly not arranged in the order in which they were written.

Some readers might also be confused by my references to gardening one day in Ashland's loamy soil, the next in Buckingham County's red clay. Truth is, John and I have two gardens—one in the small town of Ashland, where we live, the other in rural Buckingham County, where we have a cabin and an outdoor education center. Two Virginia gardens with more different growing conditions would be hard to imagine, and I credit most of my education as a gardener to what I have learned from growing plants, sometimes the same plant, in both places.

The rest of my education as a gardener, or at least the most enjoyable part of it, has come from friends and fellow gardeners. "Do you know anything about a ginger butterfly lily?" a friend asks, and although I don't at the time of the question, I do by the time we've finished chatting. What a privilege it has been to be the sounding board for so many questions and suggestions! The teacher always learns more than her students, and students of horticulture are the best of the lot.

Preface

Thanks to Jay Pace, editor of the *Herald Progress*, who published my first gardening article, to Virginia Shepherd, former editor of *Virginia Wildlife*, who launched my career in that publication not once but twice, to editor Karin Kapsidelis, who helped me make the transition from the *Herald Progress* to the *Times-Dispatch*, and to designer Mary Garner-Mitchell, who made everything I wrote for the *Times-Dispatch* look good.

Botanist John Hayden has my utmost respect and appreciation for assisting me in keeping this text botanically accurate yet readable. Where I've strayed from the party line, by calling the marigold's one-seeded fruit a seed, for example, the responsibility is mine, not his. Thanks also to my son Jay and to Cabell Harris and Tom Gibson at Work, Inc., whose initial designs for the layout of this book inspired me to pursue this project. I will consider it a great privilege if I ever have an opportunity to work professionally with such creative and generous people again.

And, finally, my biggest thanks go to my husband John, whose insightful suggestions and deep appreciation of the outdoors inform every essay in this book. To have a partner who shares one's love of gardening is one of the great blessings on earth.

January

*"A good book is like a
garden carried in the pocket."*
—ARAB PROVERB

**Turn Pages
When You
Can't Turn Soil** Every season brings a new crop of gardening books promising to make us experts on everything from growing orchids to planning landscapes, but for the most enjoyable winter reading, there's a different kind of book I would recommend.

These are the books written by gardeners who say as much about how to enjoy gardening as they do about how things grow. The best of them provide practical information (plant dahlias some time around the third week of April) along with trivia (Thomas Jefferson brought the mimosa to the south) and insight ("To be able to shut one's eyes to weeds is a great art"). Their authors tend to say "this is the way it happened" instead of "this is so," and when they describe the way they planted the primroses, they include the warmth of the sun.

Katharine White's *Onward and Upward in the Garden* (1958), Eleanor Perenyi's *Green Thoughts* (1966), and Henry Mitchell's *The Essential Earthman* (1981), all fit the bill, but so do dozens of books published earlier that you can find in the library stacks or pick up for a pittance at a used book store. As often as not, the ones I like best were published before 1950. Although some of their information is dated, their charm has increased. A book called *Old Fashioned Garden Flowers*, for example, has a certain ring of authenticity when you discover it was published in 1936. Three books you will enjoy as much as gardeners must have enjoyed them long ago are *Another Gardener's Bed Book* by Richardson Wright (1933), *Four Hedges* by Clare Leighton (1935), and *The Joyful Gardener* by Agnes Rothery (1927). *Another Gardener's Bed Book* (1933) consists of a series of entries to be read every night of the year by "those who garden by day and read by night." Most of the entries are short and range in scope from Wright's reflections on yard boys ("created for the sole purpose of doing stupid things") to lists of good names for country houses. There is also gardening advice keyed to the time of the year, and although the advice often applies to plants I don't grow, it's nice to go to bed dreaming of currant bushes.

Four Hedges is entirely different. Where Wright is pithy and erudite, Leighton is lyrical and loving. "Ours is an ordinary garden," writes Leighton. "It is perched on a slope of the Chiltern Hills, exposed to every wind that blows." Leighton describes her garden as a living thing where the doings of insects are as important as machinations of men, and no beauty is ever overlooked. *Four Hedges* is illustrated with Leighton's exquisite wood engravings, many of which are reproduced in this book.

Agnes Rothery's *The Joyful Gardener* is written by a gardener who deserves the title, but she is also a scholar and international traveler who is as well-versed in Chaucer as chard. Hers is the kind of book I take notes on, hoping to remember that *wort*, as in ragwort, is from the Anglo-Saxon *wyrt* for plant, and that *paradise*, a Persian word, originally meant an enclosed space set apart and adorned with trees.

All these books I found in used bookstores where there may be other treasures waiting to be discovered. Here are a few tips that will help you find them. First, read a few paragraphs and listen for the gardener's voice. The voice doesn't have to be lyrical, just present. Garden books written in the third person by authors who know everything are great for reference, but when I take a book to bed, I want to know who is talking. Phrases like "my blackbird" and "our beech" are good signs. So are unbridled opinions like Katharine White's "a ruffled snapdragon is an abomination" and Agnes Rothery's "membership in a garden club is more dangerous than joining the Communist Party."

Other things to look for include weather and failure. If you can flip through the book and find reference to a killing frost, a damaging wind, or a ruinous drought, you know the author is gardening in the same world you are. Reference to failure is a good sign, too. When Clare Leighton writes "the seedling grew brown and faded a few days after being put into the ground," I know she is an author I can relate to.

You may also want to thumb through to see how many plant names you can recognize. I read to learn and welcome the unfamiliar, but if every plant name in the book is something I have never heard of, either the author and I are gardening in different climates, or we're gardening at extraordinarily different levels of expertise. To enjoy reading about the sixty names for pansy, you first have to know what a pansy is.

And finally, there's one thing I've found in so many good, old, gardening books I've begun to use it as a clue. If you can find a pressed flower between the pages, consider it a rave review.

Make This the Year of the Stick

"Plant more sticks" was my gardening resolution this year, because I enjoyed using sticks so much in holiday decorations. I hadn't been aware I'd collected so many until I started retrieving them from the side porch, the utility room, the top of the wood pile. Some sticks I had saved because they were wrapped in brown braids of honeysuckle. Others I had saved because I liked their twig structure. Still others were heirloom sticks—sticks I've been using for years, ever since they were given to me by a neighbor who had cut them from her shrub called Harry Lauder's walking stick.

That's the beauty of sticks. They don't droop, wilt, or fade. A beautiful stick can be used in a Christmas arrangement, then a Valentine's Day arrangement, then an Easter arrangement. Shrubs with graceful twig structure or contorted stems also provide focal points in a winter garden. Almost any shrub or tree can be a source of interesting sticks, but some are more valuable than others because they have landscape interest as well as value to arrangers.

Harry Lauder's walking stick is the Tiffany of shrubs when it comes to providing valuable sticks. Named for Harry Lauder, a Scottish balladeer who carried a twisted walking stick with him whenever he appeared on stage, it's a medium to slow-growing shrub that has branches so gnarled and contorted they sometimes turn in on themselves like knots. Every branch of this shrub is a treasure to an arranger, and a good-sized shrub (they will grow to 10 feet) is as striking as sculpture in the winter garden. My neighbors and I are still mourning the loss of one of these shrubs that a new neighbor cut down before he knew what it was. "I tried to see if the branches were still in his yard somewhere," said one heartbroken arranger, "but they'd been carted off to the dump." Had she found them, she said she was going to put the branches in boxes like the ones long-stemmed roses come in and give them to other arrangers as gifts!

The botanical name of Harry Lauder's walking stick is *Corylus avellana* 'Contorta.' It is a cultivated variety of European filbert and will grow in full sun or part shade. Because the wood of the contorted cultivar is grafted onto understock of the European filbert, straight suckers occasionally shoot up from the roots, and these should be removed.

Other shrubs and trees are valuable for the shape of their branches, too. Corkscrew willow (*Salix matsudana* 'Tortuosa') is a wonderful fast-growing tree with gray-brown branches that spiral upward in a corkscrew pattern. Because corkscrew willows grow so much faster than Harry Lauder's walking sticks, it seems a much less monumental act to cut one of their branches than it does to cut a branch of Harry Lauder's walking stick. Last spring, when a variety store in Ashland offered corkscrew willows for sale, a particularly astute local gardener managed to convince the salesperson that, because one tree looked partially dead, its price should be lowered from the already low price of $10 to $5. Little did the salesperson know that even a dead corkscrew willow has branches worth $10 to an arranger.

The fantail or fasciated willow is another source of great sticks. The branches of this rounded shrub or small tree (*Salix sachalinensis* 'Sekka') are uniquely twisted and sometimes flat. A friend once used fasciated willow branches in an arrangement she created to interpret the swirling clouds in a Van Gogh painting at the Virginia Museum of Fine Arts, and the branches of this shrub have reminded me of Van Gogh brush strokes ever since. These willows prefer moist soils and full sun.

Finally, don't overlook the branches of our native winged elm. Seedlings of this tree, *Ulmus alata*, have flattened appendages on opposite sides of their twigs, and they, too, can be dramatic in arrangements. Winged elm seedlings come up like weeds in my yard, but cutting them down is no chore when you've got big plans for the sticks.

Cyclamen Flourish in January Dreams

The best gardens grow in January when imagination is all they need to succeed, and in mine I'm growing a drift of hardy cyclamen. They cover the ground and spill down the bank under my oak. In September they send up shimmering pink blossoms with dark magenta eyes. A month later their heart-shaped foliage appears, and they cover the ground with dark green, silver-splashed leaves.

My hardy cyclamen garden was inspired by Elizabeth Lawrence, author of *The Little Bulbs* (1957, 1986). Lawrence gardened in Raleigh and later in Charlotte, North Carolina, where she grew cyclamen and almost every other small bulb, corm, or tuber known to man. In *The Little Bulbs* she describes flowers as familiar as the spring crocus and as rare as the Lebanon squill, but it was her chapter on hardy cyclamen that captured me. Everything she said about them made them sound like a perfect choice for growing under my oak.

She described their blossoms as looking like butterflies resting for just a moment on their stems—just the kind of image I warm to, and she provided advice for the beginning cyclamen grower that I felt privileged to have. Her most important tip was to tell me which type to grow. According to Lawrence, *Cyclamen neopolitanum* (now called *C. hederifolium*) is the only truly hardy and long-lived cyclamen.

"I wish I had known years ago, when I began a collection," she wrote, "that this is the beginner's cyclamen."

She also told me how to plant them—upside down by ordinary standards. A cyclamen's roots grow from the top of the tubers, and they will not bloom if their roots are turned toward the earth at planting time.

Their other requirements include shallow planting with their roots barely covered or even partly exposed, good drainage, and humus-rich soil. Some say lime stimulates flowering, and Lawrence recommends giving the tubers an annual mulch of leaf mold mixed with wood ashes and bone meal. What they offer in return, she writes, is "bloom when bloom is most welcome" and bloom in places that need it most—the shady places beneath trees.

What appeals to me most about these hardy cyclamen, however, is their longevity and the fact that they're a long-term investment. Cyclamen can be left undisturbed for years and often outlive the person who planted them. In fact, according to Lawrence, it takes a medium-length lifetime for the tubers to grow large enough to reach their full flowering. A gardener who plants a cyclamen tuber the size of a quarter this year, she writes, can expect more than 500 blooms on the same plant when it reaches its full flowering size, but that may take 40 years.

Such slow progress might seem like an impediment in an ordinary garden, but not in a January garden. There my cyclamen have already reached maturity and are sending up myriads of pale pink blooms.

All I have to do now is plant them.

Snowdrops Melt January Hearts

Earliest came the snowdrops, pale children of the snows.
—LOUISE BEEBE WILDER

No archeologist ever brushed dirt from a shard of pottery any more carefully than I brushed snow from my snowdrops this month. I would have left them safely covered, but I wanted to photograph the hearts on the petals deep inside the flowers. Between two snowfalls, my snowdrops bloomed. They weren't in full bloom, but they were far enough out of the earth on January 30 that I could take a blossom inside and search it for that hidden heart. I knew it was there because Gertrude Jeykll said it was. Jekyll, whose garden writing has been the focus of my winter hibernation, said to look inside each flower for a tiny green heart. It appears not on what we think of as the flower's petals (the large white sepals that look like helicopter blades) but on the flower's true petals which form a tight little tube inside the showy white sepals. Turn the flower upside down (large white sepals pointing up), and you will see the tiny (¼ inch) green heart on each petal.

Snow or no snow, spring began for me on January 30 when I discovered that first snowdrop. That it came bearing a valentine was just more proof that winter stillness had ended and the thrills of spring had begun. Believe it or not, I noticed winter aconite, another very early bulb, blooming—or at least showing its bent bud, the same day, and a neighbor, Sarah Wright, reported her *Iris stylosa* were blooming. The second snow slowed spring's progress a bit, but it won't stop the show altogether. As soon as the snowdrops are up, there will be no total breaks in flowering until frosts take next fall's flowers.

Every gardener who wants spring to begin in January should grow snowdrops. If you don't know anyone who has them to share, you can order dormant bulbs in the fall and plant them then. Most bulb catalogs and local nurseries carry them. But if you do know someone who has snowdrops, start buttering him or her up now, because the best time to move snowdrops is when they are "in the green," which means after they've bloomed but while their foliage is still showing. If you are lucky enough to have snowdrops, that's also the best time to divide them. They like full sun or part shade and rich soil that is moist but well drained. The humus-rich soil under a deciduous tree is perfect.

Joanna Reed, an accomplished Pennsylvania gardener I visited one winter, showed me acres of naturalized snowdrops, the only such display I'd seen anywhere except in pictures, and I asked her how she accomplished it. When she was 65, she said, she was given her first clump of snowdrops and told to divide them "in the green" by pulling away single bulbs and planting each one in a separate hole. She was reluctant, at her age, to spread them out so thinly, so she put two bulbs in each hole. Every year she divided them that way, and at the time of my visit, when she was in her 80s, her woods were awash in white.

The only really hard thing about growing snowdrops, other than remembering to order the bulbs in the fall or talking another gardener out of some in the spring, is remembering where they are planted. Once they have gone dormant, there's nothing showing above ground to show you where they're planted and it's easy to damage them by inadvertently planting something on top of them. The best way to avoid this problem is to plant something with them that will "hold their spot" during the summer and fall. Ferns work as do shallow-rooted groundcovers like creeping phlox (*Phlox stolonifera*).

It is also supposed to be bad luck to carry the first snowdrop of the season into the house, but by all means bring the second one in because the warmth of the house will bring out its honey-like fragrance. Snowdrops don't make good cut flowers; they sort of melt (lose substance), but in January a melting snowdrop hanging over the edge of a cup is as glorious as a vase of peonies in May.

Avoiding Avalanche Damage

Sometime before the gutters collapsed and the snow crashed down off the roof, I was praising the virtues of snow. "Great insulation for the plants," I commented to a neighbor. "A good source of water for the grass," I pointed out to my husband. For as much snow as we'd had, there seemed surprisingly little damage from it, and the most apparent evidence that we'd been through unusual weather was a bumper crop of gum balls on the ground. That, as I said, was before the avalanche.

Crrrash! Two feet of snow rushing headlong off a high-pitched roof onto the rhododendron below.

Why, oh why, did we plant the rhododendron there? It

wasn't just that we had planted it there. We had actually *moved* it there from another part of the yard. A safe place, I realize now. The rhododendron was at least 5 feet tall when John and I decided we could move it. It took half a day to dig a hole big enough to accommodate it; it took another half a day to dig it up and work a tarp under it so that we could drag it inch by inch to the hole. It was good work, the best we could have done, and although we were not entirely surprised that the shrub survived, we were truly complimented when it thrived. This spring would have been its most glorious year. But for the snow.

Of such painful lessons are gardening educations made. Never again will I fail to take into account the pitch of the roof when locating a shrub below.

The lesson is learned, but already I find myself wondering if this year wasn't just an unusual one. With less accumulation and "average" snowfalls wouldn't my rhododendron have been safe?

The question is moot. Garden plants don't grow under average weather conditions. It is the extremes of heat and cold, the maximum and minimum rainfalls, the record accumulations of snow that set the limits on what survives. Five years of mild winters may lure us into believing a camellia is as hardy as a holly, then comes a record cold to even things out. So much for the camellia. I recently read that it's not snow accumulation per se but the moisture content of snow that determines how damaging snow is to foundation plantings (foundations plantings are the ones up close to the house). Hydrologists compute the ratio of the number of inches of snow that falls in a given storm to the number of inches of water that snow will produce; the lower the ratio, the heavier the snow and the more damage it will do shrubs. New England snow reportedly usually has a low ratio (10 inches of snow on average yield 1 inch of water). The eastern slope of the Rockies, on the other hand, has powdery snow (50 inches of snow may yield only 1 inch of water.)

John Newell, who mans Ashland's weather station, says the

snow in our central Virginia community typically also has a ten to one ratio. That is, 10 inches of snow yield about 1 inch of water. Although he doesn't have a measurement to confirm it, he believes that the snow that took out my rhododendron was unusually heavy and wet. Based on the number of hand squeezes it took to make a snowball, I'd agree.

There are many strategies for preventing such heavy, wet snows from damaging foundation plantings. Our neighbors the Flippos have wonderful lathe cages they put over their box-woods to break the fall of the snow. The Joneses on South Center Street protect their azaleas with 2 by 4s propped diagonally against the house. Until this year's snowfall, I had thought they were using the 2 by 4s to prop up the house. In the northeast, many homeowners encircle upright shrubs with twine to keep their limbs from drooping under the weight of the snow.

I doubt the majority of Virginia gardeners will ever take snow seriously enough to adopt such strategies, but they might employ the simpler technique of supporting broadleaf evergreens like rhododendrons and mountain laurels with evergreen boughs tucked between their branches. According to garden writer Gordon Hayward, this creates a springy cushion that makes the shrub more resilient to the weight of rooftop avalanche.

An even better strategy is not to plant shrubs that can be easily damaged by snow in an avalanche zone. Azaleas that looked beautiful when you planted them right under the dripline of your roof in April look like sitting ducks when it snows. For aesthetic reasons, many landscapers are moving away from the traditional line of evergreen shrubs planted close to the house anyway; they are designing wider, more naturalistic beds, so a gardener needn't feel his house is naked without an apron of Japanese holly around the foundation. Garden-designer Margaret Hensel says that where snow is a problem, borders can be 6 to 10 feet wide, extending into the area that was once typically lawn. Shrubs and perennials can be set into this bed informally, leaving a gap between shrubs and the area into which snow falls from the roof. Some plants can also handle a snowslide better than others. Perennials like peonies, for example, will die to the ground in winter but create a shrubby effect in spring and summer. Hostas and many ferns also stay out of harm's way by dying back in winter. For shrubs planted under the eaves, Gordon Hayward recommends those that are naturally prostrate like junipers and Leucothoe, those that are resilient like Shrubby St. John's wort (*Hypericum prolificum*) and mugo pine, and those that bloom on new wood like some hydrangeas and butterfly bush, because these, even if they are damaged by snow, will recover in time to flower the following summer.

All this is scant consolation to the gardener mourning the loss of his prized rhododendron, but it's something to think about when choosing our replacement plants in the spring.

February

Windowsill Gardening

If you think you can't order too many seeds in January, wait until February when you've decided to start a few of them in the house. February is to seed flats as bathing suits are to inches—the further you get into the former, the more you wish you had fewer of the latter. Fortunately, at least with seed flats, this effect can be somewhat controlled.

First of all, don't start anything in the house unless you have to. The uncontrollable urge to see something growing is a perfectly good reason to "have to," but don't forget you will still be tending those seed flats in March when the daffodils are glorious outside. Seeds of warm-season annuals will be happier, and a lot less hassle, planted outside when the ground is warm than if they languish on winter windowsills. The only seeds I really feel justified in starting inside are seeds of plants difficult to germinate outside, seeds of plants that I want to harvest at the earliest possible date, and seeds of plants that need a jump-start to bring them to blooming size by their spring blooming times.

How, then, do I explain the dozens of jiffy pots, flats, and egg cartons containing seeds that could just as well have been started outside in May perched on my windowsills right now? My explanation will be familiar to every gardener who has ever placed a flat in front of a window on top of a radiator: "I couldn't wait."

You can never have enough windowsills for the seeds you want to start in the winter. According to the First Law of Windowsill Gardening, there are always half as many available windowsills as there are desired seed flats. Further divide that by the number of windowsills that receive adequate sunlight, and the seed flats multiply to infinity. I state this law with some authority as the owner of a house with sixteen windows on the south side (count them; my husband, who painted them, has), and whose husband (same one) has just built a table and indoor lighting assembly to hold the overflow flats.

Actually, I intend the indoor lighting arrangement eventually to replace the windowsills altogether. That would mean, I hope: no more moving the TV tables that hold the seed flats back and forth every night when I want to close the blinds, no more wondering where the TV tables are when I want to use them as they were intended, and no more seedlings with sickly white stems reaching for the light. For, no matter how much light comes in the window in February (and I heard a recent report that there is an average of only thirteen sunny days in February), there's never enough. Either you were late for work and forgot to open the curtains, or the soil settled in the flat and the seedlings couldn't see, much less sunbathe, over the sides. By the beginning of March, I want to take the roof off the house and replace the sides with glass, an invention which I believe is known as a greenhouse but which is otherwise known only in my dreams.

The best substitute, I think, is my new growing-table with lights. The table itself is constructed of a 3- by 6-foot plywood sheet set on metal legs. It will accommodate six 11- by 21-inch flats. Above the table, from a 60-inch-long by 36-inch-wide by 36-inch-high frame of 2 by 4s, hang four shop-light assemblies each of which holds two 48-inch, 40-watt fluorescent tubes. There is wasted space at each end of the table, but the table is the right size to serve as a picnic table when the seedlings graduate.

The light assemblies hang by chains from the wooden frame, and the chains allow the lights to be raised as the seedlings grow. In each of the light assemblies are two cool-white fluorescent tubes, although I have read that one cool-white and one warm-white tube create a light mix most beneficial to indoor plants. Seedlings, for sure, do not need the special wide spectrum lights sold as "Grow Lights" that can be eight times as expensive as the ordinary tubes. Those lights give off enough light at the red end of the spectrum to trigger flowering, but by the time seedlings are ready for flowering, they should be outdoors.

The type of light for seedlings is probably less important than its intensity. The bulbs should stay about 6 inches above the plants and should stay on for about 16 hours a day. My guess is that ideally I should have two more tubes illuminating my own table, but I'll wait to see how the seedlings do before installing them.

After all, what with the flats, the table, the tubes, and the light assemblies (not to mention the water, the electricity, and the elbow grease), we have invested pretty heavily in our seeds this year. Only a few of them have come up. And, of course, by now, so have the daffodils.

Spring Guests Arrive Early

Every bloom in the month of February is worth ten in the month of June. In fact, there may not be enough marigolds all summer to equal the first spring crocus.

Ornamentals that bloom in late winter or very early spring are like the first guests to arrive at a party; there's time to enjoy them before all the commotion begins.

The earliest guests in our garden each year are usually the snowdrops (*Galanthus nivalis*). This year our first snowdrops bloomed before the end of January, and some of them are still blooming now, almost a month later. Because they bloom so very early, you would expect them to come in wearing heavy overcoats or at least looking woolly, but there is nothing quite so delicate-looking as the white, drooping petals of a snowdrop.

Winter aconite (*Eranthis hyemalis*) are usually next to arrive in the garden. These buttercup-yellow flowers are only about 1½ inches across and 2 to 3 inches tall, but they create a big splash of color where they have naturalized. I used to wonder why they weren't as popular as crocuses because I found them easier to grow than crocuses because squirrels don't eat them. But I've learned that my success with winter aconite is unusual and due, in part, to the fact that I obtained my tubers "fresh" from a neighbor and not dried out from a mail-order source.

Crocuses arrive next at the party. Coaxed out by the sun in early February, my yellow crocuses have been waiting for equally warm days ever since. Stalwart they've stood through the rain and snow, wishing, I'm sure, that they could go back where they came from like the groundhog.

Some crocuses bloom earlier than others no matter where you plant them, but you can hurry them all up a bit by planting them on a south facing slope or on the south side of a house where they'll warm up as early as possible in the spring. It also makes sense to plant them near the house or driveway so that you don't have to walk far to see them; I find myself trying to tiptoe weightless across the winter-wet lawn to visit my crocus without compacting the soil.

Blooming in the garden now, too, is the Lenten rose (*Helleborus orientalis*). More closely related to the buttercup than the rose, this plant took my breath away the first time I saw it blooming in the Mews on Richmond's Church Hill. On an icy winter day, when flowers seemed out of the question, its blossoms seemed as ethereal as ghosts. Now I know this is a ghost with an iron constitution, because not only do its flowers brave the cold, they seem to last forever. Once, after a warm December, I recorded my first Lenten rose blooming on January 3, and I still had respectable-looking Lenten roses blooming at the beginning of May.

The Lenten rose's 3-inch-wide flowers range in color from cream to light green and a muted, reddish purple. Borne several to a 6- to 12-inch stalk, they're often partially hidden by the plant's umbrella-like, evergreen foliage, but they are visible enough to make a show. In a congenial spot (partial shade with rich, moist soil) they will self-sow, but it takes a while to get a good-sized colony going, so count it a treasure if a friend gives you one.

There are other early guests in the garden, but they are mostly uninvited. A dandelion sparkles in the middle of the lawn, a chickweed flaunts its blossoms by the door. All the guests are atwitter, though, about the arrival of the guest of honor. The first daffodil is blooming near the downspout.

So let the celebration begin!

Winter Bulb Gets Stamp of Approval

I knew one of my favorite winter flowers had made it into the big leagues when it appeared on a first class stamp. It was a surprise to see it there because I didn't think many people knew about it, but if your image appears on a first-class stamp, how unknown can you be? Then I realized why winter aconite was receiving such wide exposure: along with better-known crocus, pansy, snowdrop, and anemone, it was part of the U.S. Postal Service's "Garden Flowers" series, and this series of five stamps was to represent winter flowers. That certainly explains winter aconite's selection—

there are only so many winter flowers to choose from, and winter aconite not only fits the bill, it's photogenic.

One might argue about whether all the flowers in this series are really winter flowers; pansies will bloom off and on all winter, but I don't think of them as winter flowers, and tuberous anemones (windflowers) bloom in early spring. But winter aconite is truly a winter flower.

This year, my winter aconite emerged from the ground on January 30. Then it snowed. About two hundred of them were blooming on February 10. Then it snowed again. And now, having survived two snowfalls and sub-freezing temperatures, they are all up and blooming—a low carpet of buttercup-yellow flowers brightening an otherwise winter-weary yard. The fact that I had little to do with the creation of this carpet does nothing to diminish my pride in it. I was lucky, planted the original clump of tubers in the right place, and they have spread by seed to cover an area about as big as a good-sized living room rug. Any such expanse of self-sown flowers would be exciting, but one that blooms in winter is downright thrilling.

I'm going to tell you every detail I know about how to grow these flowers, because they chase the winter doldrums better than any plant I know, and unless you do it by accident, as I did, it's hard to succeed with them. They need to be planted at the right time, in the right way, and in the right place.

Mine came from a neighbor—that was the first strike in their favor. "It is difficult to establish a new colony of it unless you can rob an old one," I read later in Elizabeth Lawrence's *The Little Bulbs*. That's because the tubers dry out quickly and suffer from being kept out of the ground too long. They are best moved "in the green," which means before the foliage has disappeared. You can even move them while they're flowering, which is what I did.

But what if you don't have a neighbor with winter aconite? Then you have to buy the tubers from a nursery or mail-order source. Buy them as early as you can from the most reputable dealer you know, and plant them as soon as they arrive. To keep them from drying out, bulb growers coat the tiny tubers in wax, but they are still likely to be desiccated when they arrive in the fall. Experts recommend soaking them overnight to rehydrate them. Even then, says one experienced gardener, you'll be lucky if a fifth of your tubers sprout.

That sounds discouraging, but it's not as bad as it sounds, because if you can establish only a couple of plants in a spot they like, they will set seed and spread. That is, unless you've bought the species the U.S. Postal Service says is depicted on its new stamp. That one, *Eranthis* × *Tubergenii*, is a sterile hybrid you don't want, unless you don't want your winter aconite to set seed, which would be like not wanting your mail to arrive. The winter aconite you want is *Eranthis hyemalis*. Its flowers are a little smaller than those of *Eranthis* × *Tubergenii*, but it is easier to grow and it will set seed.

As inspiration for your winter aconite growing, here are two images to keep in mind. One is of 10 acres of winter aconite. That's what Brent Heath, owner of the Daffodil Mart, said he saw once at Cincinnati's Spring Grove Cemetery. The other is of a woodland described in a letter to Elizabeth Lawrence: "If you don't like yellow, you won't like the woods now," her friend wrote. "There are tens of thousands of winter aconite in bloom, so thick that one can see them a hundred yards away. I love to see the patches of color repeat themselves in the distance. Here is a plant that is very permanent, as I have my original plantings that must be more than fifty years old. They grow bigger and seem better every year. All of the other patches came from seeds, simply strewn on the ground without any preparation."

Although I have never deliberately spread the seeds of my winter aconite, I think I may do it inadvertently when I weed around the mature plants. After the flowers fade, light brown papery pods appear above the plant's ruffed foliage, and they spill their seeds in early May. Soon after, the foliage yellows and disappears, but there is a period of a few weeks between the flowers' blooming and the foliage's yellowing when these deeply cut leaves alone are ornamental. Rising on 3- to 4-inch stems, they look like Lilliputian palm trees, and I like to keep them weeded to show them off.

Brent Heath gave me another tip on how to grow winter aconite. He told me many gardeners fail with their original tubers because they plant them too deep, and he recommends planting them no more than an inch deep.

The plants like part shade and are said to prefer moist, humus-rich soil. Unlike most bulbs that positively abhor wet feet, these tiny tubers actually like damp conditions, but mine do fine in the relatively dry soil under a greedy Norway maple. The shade of a deciduous tree suits them because they've finished their active growth by the time the trees leaf out.

Another thing they like is a spot to themselves where they won't be disturbed and where they'll have some bare ground into which their seeds can spread. This makes siting them a little tricky, because their foliage totally disappears when they go dormant and that leaves a hole where they grew in the winter and spring. A groundcover that doesn't crowd them too much, like native *Phlox stolonifera*, will hold their spot without outcompeting them, but during the years when my winter aconite were getting established, they were pretty much alone in their bed.

And finally, they need time. "This isn't an instant gratification plant," said Heath "You've got to be patient." I planted my first clump about 15 years ago, so it hasn't become a carpet overnight. On the other hand, these things grow exponentially, so my rug-sized patch might be room-sized next year.

Two Routes to February Daffodils

It's not often that Conde Hopkins's dirt pile and Mary Pauli's coffee table have something in common, but this month they do: blooming daffodils.

The Hopkins' daffodils are blooming on the south side of a pile of topsoil that was never moved because the children appropriated it for dinosaur maneuvers. The Paulis' daffodils are blooming in a pot on the coffee table because Mary did what she needed to do to trick them into thinking it was time to bloom. Both are treasures during the month of February when a fresh flower is worth its weight in gold. How did they do it?

The Hopkins didn't even plant the daffodils that came up on the side of their dirt pile—they probably rode in on the dump truck—but had they planted them with the intention of having them bloom early, they could not have done a better job. Not only do the Hopkins' daffodils grow on the south side of the dirt pile where the dirt captures and keeps the warmth of the sun, they are an old, early-blooming variety. The combination of these two things—a southern exposure and an early-blooming variety like 'February Gold'—will ensure you the earliest possible outdoor daffodils. The Hopkins' first daffodil bloomed on February 12.

Although it's only the middle of February, Mary Pauli has been enjoying bulbs inside for weeks. Her *Iris reticulata* bloomed in the middle of January, her 'Barrett Browning' daffodils bloomed the end of January, her 'Monte Carlo' tulips started blooming around the first week in February, and there are enough pots of bulbs still growing in her kitchen to keep her in fresh flowers for weeks.

How does she do it?

First of all, she orders bulbs described as suitable for forcing from her bulb catalogs, because some bulbs are easier to force than others. The Dutch Gardens catalog, for example, marks bulbs that are easiest to force, with a star. The Daffodil Mart publishes a Forcer's List of daffodils and other bulbs that are particularly amenable to forcing.

For the beginner, paperwhite narcissus are a no-fail choice; they don't need to be forced, they need only be "allowed" to bloom indoors. But Pauli succeeds with more challenging daffodils like 'Barrett Browning,' 'Ice Follies,' and 'Tête-à-tête.'

Says Pauli: "I plant the bulbs as soon as I get them in

October. They [the experts] say you should use pots as wide as they are tall, but this year I didn't have any so I used what I had." Bulb growers also recommend using pots with drain holes, because bulbs can rot if the soil stays too wet, but when nothing else is available, Pauli uses pots without drain holes and waters sparingly.

Although most experts recommend potting soil for forced bulbs, Pauli plants her bulbs in garden soil mixed with compost. The best growing medium is one that stays moist but doesn't get muddy. In her soil-compost mix, Pauli arranges her bulbs so that their tips barely show at the top of the soil. Then she waters them and lets the pots drain.

"Then I put them on the back porch in an old blanket chest and ignore them for three months," she says.

According to Pauli, bucket benches like the ones many homeowners have on their porches would work just as well. The object is to store the bulbs in a place that is cold and dark. Pauli's daughter's 50°F wine cellar, she discovered, was too warm, especially for tulips, which can be finicky to force.

During the winter Pauli checks the bulbs periodically to make sure they haven't completely dried out. If they have, she gives them water. After three months, she starts checking to see if they've started to show growth. When their foliage is up 1½ to 2 inches, she brings them in the house.

The bulbs' foliage is nearly white when they emerge from the blanket chest, so she has to get them adjusted to light. For a day or two, she keeps them back from the window, then she moves them to a sunny windowsill (southern or eastern exposure) after their leaves green-up.

"I water them with a half-strength houseplant fertilizer and turn them around every day or so, so they don't lean out the window. And that's about it."

The beauty of Pauli's daffodils makes them seem well worth the trouble of forcing them to bloom. Besides, although daffodils may seem easier to grow on the side of an outdoor dirt pile, four days after the Hopkins' daffodils bloomed, they were buried in snow.

It never snows on Pauli's coffee table.

A Tiller for Lightweights

When Larry Gilman woke up one morning last week, he thought he heard a chain saw buzzing in the backyard. Had his wife Brenda gone out early to fell a few trees? No, she had borrowed my little garden tiller, a Mantis, and was doing a little tilling before heading for the office.

Ah, the luxury of it: to be able to till before work, on your lunch hour, or whenever the spirit moves you. To be able to break ground without waiting for someone with more muscle to do it for you: this is the beauty of a Mantis.

Mantis is the brand name of a tiller so small a child could use it. Green Machine, Troy-Bilt Speedy Hoe, and Hoffco Li'l Hoe are brand names of similar small tillers. They are all lightweight. My Mantis weighs only 20 pounds and has a handle that makes it easy to carry around. It's easy to start, easy to maneuver, and surprisingly powerful for such a small machine.

A Mantis is to a full-sized tiller what a dust buster is to a vacuum cleaner; the smaller tool won't do what the big one will, but for some jobs it is so much more convenient to use, you begin to think it's indispensable. I use my Mantis to extend borders where I have already turned the soil over once with a shovel and to cultivate previously tilled areas. I can use it to break new ground if the new ground is friable and nearly root less, but I wouldn't try to use it to plow a large new vegetable garden. The Mantis doesn't plow either as deeply or as wide a swath as a full-sized tiller would; it tills 6 to 8 inches deep and at a width of about 9 inches. (Against my advice, my son did use my Mantis to till a new 18- by 24-foot vegetable garden. His plot proves it can be done, but then you could vacuum the house with a dust buster, too.)

The Mantis has two pairs of tines (metal "wheels" with angled teeth) that revolve to till the soil, and you are supposed to pull the machine backwards through the soil to make it dig. The author of an article I once read comparing small tillers found walking backwards with the Mantis awkward, but when I use the Mantis, I don't really walk backwards all the time; sometimes I just pull the machine back as the tines work their way forward.

The Mantis has a two-cycle engine which means you have to mix gas and oil in the right proportions to feed it. That's a hassle (especially if, as I do, you have a lawn mower with a two-cycle engine that requires a different gas-oil mix), but get yourself a new gas can, mark it "Mantis," and prepare to feel like a budding small equipment mechanic as your shed fills up with the tools—and cans—of your trade.

The only thing I really don't like about using my Mantis is having to stop to free the tines of roots and rocks in difficult soil. A tangle of roots will stop the motion of the tines in a heartbeat, and a rock hung up between the tines and the body of the tiller will stop your progress cold. You have to pull out the cotter pin and take the tines off to clear the obstruction.

Expense is the Mantis's other drawback. A Mantis costs about $300, but the longer I have mine, the more uses I find for it and the more I value what it can do. Although I haven't tried them, attachments allow you to convert the Mantis into a border edger, lawn aerator, and lawn dethatcher. Still, it's the kind of tool no neighborhood needs more than one of, so I'd recommend having neighbors pitch in and buy one for the entire block. That way you can take turns waking each other to the sound of early morning tilling.

Mole Solutions Abound

I know this subject inside out. In fact, some of its insides are sitting on my doormat right now.

I'm referring to the insides of the eastern mole that appear as regularly as the newspaper on our front porch. They are gifts from our cats who lay them at our doorstep as offerings. Rumor has it that our newspaper boy particularly likes delivering our paper because there is always something dead to look at on our stoop. This is a distinction to which we never aspired, but since there's no denying it, we might as well make the best of it. The best of it is that our cats keep the moles in our yard under control. Now and then a mole run pops up in the lawn, but it's seldom extensive, and, as far as I know, I've never lost bulbs to moles or voles. (For what happens when the family cat dies, see "A Temporary Truce with Voles.")

It seems that everyone knows by now that voles, not moles, do most of the garden damage. Moles make the tunnels; voles come behind them and gobble up your bulbs and girdle your azaleas. Moles eat mostly animal matter (grubs, insects, earthworms); voles eat plant matter and are much more numerous than moles. These facts have been so widely publicized by the Extension Service that gardeners repeat them like a catechism. Woe be unto him who confuses moles with voles. John Elsley, plantsman for Wayside Gardens, was nearly shouted down by a roomful of gardeners one day as he was about to confuse moles with voles. On the weight of a single consonant, he almost lost all of his credibility—and this from a roomful of people who had probably never seen either animal.

Consensus like that makes me uncomfortable, so just to confuse the issue, let me add a few tidbits of information. Analysis of moles' stomachs has shown them to contain a small percentage of "plant fibers and rootlets, seed pods and husks, and skin of grain or roots." These might have been accidentally ingested as the mole went after invertebrates, you say? That's what scientists thought too, until new evidence emerged suggesting moles may, occasionally, feed on some plant matter. Granted, moles aren't cut out to be vegetarians (they have the wrong kind of teeth and digestive systems), but there's enough evidence they eat a little plant matter to suggest they shouldn't be absolved of all plant crimes. Just the tunnels they make around roots will sometimes dry roots out.

On the other hand, there are good things moles do for the lawn and garden besides eat some harmful insects. Dr. John Pagels, mammologist at Virginia Commonwealth University, says moles till and aerate the soil. "I was trying to grow grass on hardpan until the moles came through and really worked the soil," he says. "Now the areas the moles worked over are the ones growing the best grass." And Dr. Pagels isn't the only gardener I've heard say he uses mole runs almost as one would an irrigation system. "When the moles tunnel under my bean plants, I put the hose in their burrows and let the water spread through them," he says.

More often, however, either because the runs themselves are troublesome or because plant-eating voles are using them, gardeners are trying to get rid of moles, and here are some of the more humane ways I've heard suggested for doing it. The first two presume moles will eat enough plant matter to do themselves in, a questionable presumption, but we won't quibble.

Growing gopher purge (*Euphorbia lathyris*) is one suggested remedy. The acrid taste of the plant's roots is supposed to turn moles away. Horticulturists at Carroll Gardens recommend planting gopher purge 10 inches apart to discourage moles and gophers, but I don't see how you could ring an entire vegetable garden with it without enormous effort, and a perennial bed ringed with gopher purge would hardly be a thing of beauty. I have grown this plant, and it's a tall, ungainly biennial I had no interest in growing again once I'd seen what it looked like.

Castor beans are another recommended mole solution. "We call that mole plant," Miles Holt said when he saw me growing castor beans in my garden. I grow castor beans for their ornamental value. Their big, reddish, palmate leaves look downright tropical (no surprise there; the plant is from the tropics), but Holt says if you drop the beans in the mole tunnels, the moles will eat them, get diarrhea, and die. This is the flip side of the Juicy Fruit solution. Pieces of Juicy Fruit gum strategically placed in mole runs where the moles will eat them are supposed to kill moles by giving them constipation. In addition to their gastrointestinal effects, castor beans might actually kill the moles outright, since the beans are poisonous to humans.

Then there is the nifty Mole Evictor. This is a product sold in the Plow and Hearth mail order catalog that promises, in fact *guarantees*, "to rid your lawn and garden of moles, voles, and other underground bulldozers." It's a battery-powered contraption that sends out vibrations into the soil and causes moles to abandon their burrows when they feel the shock waves and sense danger. It's supposed to be effective up to 500 square feet, and Steve Wagner, in charge of product development for Plow and Hearth, says he has used it himself and it works. I was less than impressed with the research he told me was done by the German manufacturer, but if it doesn't work, Plow and Hearth will return your money. All $99 of it.

If none of these solutions works, may I suggest a cat? Anyone willing to pay $99 for a mole evictor, see me on the price of a kitten.

Tribute to a Trowel

I suppose a carpenter feels about his favorite hammer the way I feel about my digger. It's not just my favorite tool, it's my most treasured possession. There is no object I spend more time with and none that gives me more pleasure.

Clearly, this is no ordinary trowel. It's a 22-inch steel digging implement with a pointed blade about 3 inches wide, a long handle, and a molded red rubber grip. I bought it five years ago from Brent Heath of the Daffodil Mart when he came to speak to the Ashland Garden Club. He had brought along about five of them which he sold for $5 each. Best $5 I ever spent.

Not only is it stronger than most hand trowels, my digger is longer which gives it more leverage. I've used it for every job in the garden that requires anything less than a shovel. Using an ordinary hand trowel feels like trying to dig with a spoon after using my heavy-duty digger.

I hadn't had it more than a month when I realized what a prize it was. Fearing I might lose it, I wrote Brent Heath and asked if I might buy another. To my dismay, he said he didn't sell them any more. Suddenly my digger was not only a treasure, it was irreplaceable. Misplacing it became cause for major concern. "I can't come in until I've found my digger," I told my family more than once. You'd think such a large implement with a red grip would be hard to lose, but no tool is too conspicuous to be lost by an absent-minded gardener.

My worst fear was realized one day when a friend and I went on a wildflower rescue mission. Immediately before the Slash Cottage property was to be developed as a subdivision, Betty Lottimer and I contacted the owners and asked permission to remove some of the wild iris (*Iris verna*) about to be bull-dozed. They said yes, and I was carrying a bucket full of wild iris out of the Slash Cottage woods when I realized my digger must have fallen out of the bucket.

Since Betty was a new friend, I tried not to behave like a child who had lost her favorite toy, but Betty read me too well. She said she had a shovel she felt that way about herself! She even offered to help me retrace our steps and take time to make a thorough search of where we'd been. Searching the Slash Cottage woods for my digger was like combing Sherwood Forest for an arrow, but Betty had a tracker's eye and led us back over every step of ground we'd visited. Finally, behind one of hundreds of highbush blueberries we'd passed, Betty spotted my digger.

There are dozens of other virtues for which I've learned to appreciate Betty Lottimer, but she will always have special status among my friends as The Person Who Found My Digger.

Not long after nearly losing it, I decided to show my digger to a metal worker in the hope he might be able to make me another one if I ever lost it. But that turned out to be unnecessary, because a week later my husband came home from work like a conquering hero and pointed to a picture in a catalog. My digger!

"Is this the Garden Tool you are looking for???" read the headline, uncanny in its accuracy, in the Walt Nicke catalog. Pictured below the headline, like an inventory of answered prayers, was a whole line of heavy-duty trowels designed just like mine and available in a variety of lengths. For a 22-inch model like mine, the price had gone up: Now the best digger in the world was $12, but the insurance such a purchase would offer me seemed a bargain at twice that price. I whipped out my checkbook and ordered two.

March

Pilgrimage for Pansies   It may be gardens at Winterthur, Dumbarton Oaks, and Monticello that most gardeners want to imitate, but in March, I want a garden that looks like the sidewalk in front of our local grocery store.

That's where they keep their pansies.

Never do pansies look more spectacular than when they are crowded together in flats where they can look each other straight in the eye. For these assemblages alone, one of my favorite garden tours of the year is my annual pilgrimage to garden centers to buy pansies.

My first stop this year took me to a garden center where I nearly swooned when I walked into a room full of pansy flats. Somebody had forgotten to open the greenhouse vent, which was a momentary crisis for the man in charge but a rare straight shot of pansy perfume for me. The pansies were beautiful, the fragrance irresistible, and I bought some.

My favorites are the solid-colored small ones, the bicolored small ones, the solid-colored large ones, the multicolored large ones, the yellow and black ones, the lavender-pink ones, the velvety purple ones, the rose-purple ones with darker faces, the mahogany ones, the solid yellow ones, the blue ones, the white ones, . . . etc. Oh, and tricolored Johnny-jump-ups, I really love those. Just because I already had Johnny-jump-ups popping up like weeds in my borders didn't prevent me from buying some of the more vigorous-looking ones from the nursery.

Next, I went looking for 'Chantreyland' violas. I have a feeling the distinction between pansies and violas has been obscured as hybridizers have had their way with these flowers. Technically, they all belong to the genus *Viola*, but the flowers I call violas have solid color faces, relatively small flowers, and greater heat tolerance than garden pansies. Although I usually like flowers to stay in the colors that are traditional for them, I particularly like 'Chantreyland' because its outrageous orange flowers jazz up flower arrangements, and it seems particularly heat-tolerant in the garden. So when I found them, of course, I bought some.

Pansies and violas are easy to grow, and they are really best planted in the fall. If you forget to plant them in the fall, you can plant them outdoors as early as February, because they're cold-hardy. Planted in the fall, they will not only be well-established by spring, but will provide you with a few wonderfully welcome blooms through the winter.

For me, the only problem with planting pansies in the fall is that it doesn't stop me from buying them again in the spring. When I see the gargantuan pansies blooming in nurseries and garden centers in the spring, they seem to bear no relation to the fall-planted pansies in my yard. By April my fall-planted pansies will look better than the nursery-grown ones offered in the spring, but in March I can't resist those big blooms.

This year, most of the pansies for sale seem to be in peak condition, but sometimes they're old and leggy, and those you want to avoid. Buy the youngest, most compact plants you can find, not the flat with the most blooms. When they get leggy in the yard, pinch them way back and you should get another flush of bloom.

They like rich, moist soil, light shade, and cool weather. They also love to be picked and will bloom better if you don't allow them to go to seed. This is a perfect job for children because nothing appeals to a child more than a handful of pansies, and no flower holds better in a fat little fist.

They should be planted 8 inches apart, but I worked for a florist once who told me to cram as many into every basket as I could. At the time I thought this was pansy abuse, but now I think he may have had the right idea. Buy pansies by the hundreds, mix them up like the colors in a kaleidoscope, jam them together like sardines, and you may get a display almost as nice as the one in front of my local grocery store.

A Taste for Weeds

Anyone who says he actually likes weeding . . . either lies or has deficient powers to discriminate between what is irksome and what is pleasurable.

—ALLEN LACY, *Home Ground*

Hold on there, Mr. Lacy. Surely you don't mean there's no pleasure in pulling bitter cress in March, because nothing could be further from the truth. Every gardener has favorite weeds (Sara Stein even wrote a book about hers called *My Weeds*), and in March my favorite is hairy bitter cress.

You know this weed. It forms little 3- to 5-inch-wide rosettes of cress-like leaves with upright stalks topped by tiny white flowers; each flower is about the size of a hyphen on a keyboard. In March you'll find it almost anywhere there's a spot of bare earth from which its annual seeds can sprout, but the place I enjoy seeing it most is around early, old-fashioned daffodils. Bitter cress blooming at the base of old daffodils is as ubiquitous a combination as baby's breath with long stemmed red roses, and to my eye, the former is more beautiful.

True, I don't love bitter cress so much that I'm willing to let it smother my fire pinks, but it's a plant I enjoy getting up close and personal with as I weed. It's an obliging little plant, easy to pull out even from cold, wet soil, and a big pile of it makes me feel ever so industrious. Bitter cress will even entertain you.

Its performance is a seed launching worthy of NASA. The stage is set for it when the bitter cress's stems elongate, seed pods lengthen, and seeds mature. What was formerly a quiet little plant becomes an explosion about to happen, because if you happen to touch one of these pods—or a dozen of them at once, as a weeding hand is likely to do—the outer covering of the pod curls up like a spring and catapults seeds at you. It's quite a phenomenon, and not without danger to gardeners' eyes.

Bitter cress offers taste treats, too. "Eat it for nursery tea between two bits of bread and butter," wrote Gertrude Jekyll about the roots of this plant in her book *Children and Gardens*. Sure enough, if you carefully wash the roots of bitter cress, you'll find that there's one relatively thick root at the center of all those fibrous ones and its flesh has a pleasant, peppery taste. From each plant you'll get about as much edible root as you do nectar from a single honeysuckle blossom, so don't expect to make many of those bread-butter-and-cress-root sandwiches without thousands of cress plants. On the other hand, Jekyll suggests to children that if they eat bitter cress roots they may acquire the plant's quality of persistence, so maybe harvesting enough cress roots to make a sandwich is a way of guaranteeing that outcome.

A good microscope will reveal another interesting thing about hairy bitter cress. I discovered it when I needed confirmation of my bitter cress's botanical name. Although all the evidence I could gather suggested my bitter cress was *Cardamine hirsuta*, the name itself (*hirsuta* meaning hairy) didn't seem to apply to the seemingly smooth stems and leaves of my plants.

Even with a magnifying glass I couldn't find any hairs, so I took my little weed to botanist Bruce King at Randolph-Macon College, and he put it under a dissecting microscope. There they were—hairy projections—very few and very small, along the leaf stalks.

There's more to be learned from pulling up weeds like bitter cress, too. In the same way that settlers examined the dirt on the roots of upturned trees to determine its fertility, gardeners can "read" the soil on weeds. When I pull a weed from a flower bed, the way it emerges and the nature of the soil it brings with it provide me information about things like the texture and moisture content of my soil. And although Allen Lacy objects to weeding because it's repetitive, I would argue that it is unchanging, seasonal activities like pulling bitter cress that give us touchstones against which to measure the significant changes in our gardens. There's nothing ambiguous about weeds; they demand to be weeded. There's no nail-biting involved in pulling weeds as there is doing weighty things such as moving plants or—terror of terrors—fertilizing. Pulling weeds can be as satisfying as doing the laundry, because there is usually no question that it needs to be done.

Besides, gardening without weeding would be like dining without food. What is gardening but encouraging plants we want and discouraging those we don't? Whether what you're pulling out is crabgrass or phlox volunteers, you're weeding. Pulling weeds, especially weeds like bitter cress, can delight the senses, exercise the body, soothe the psyche, and stimulate the intellect. In my book, that's not irksome; it's fun.

A Temporary Truce with Voles

I knew my husband had something in his hand by the mischievous look in his eye.

"You've got an animal; is it a snake?" I asked, as usual.

Then he showed me: It was a pine

vole he had found vacationing in 18 inches of compost as he turned the pile.

What was so exciting about his discovery was that I have been fighting voles for years without ever seeing one. Moles, yes; cats used to deposit them on the back stoop for us, but I had never seen a vole alive or dead. Moles eat mostly animal matter—things like worms and insect larvae—and their tunnels, which produce raised ridges, cause lawn damage, but vegetarian voles are the real scourge to gardeners. "Voles live on plant parts," reads the copy in a Virginia Cooperative Extension Service publication on controlling voles in Virginia, but what that prosaic statement means to a gardener is that lily and tulip bulbs disappear overnight, small trees, especially fruit trees, become girdled, and established shrubs that looked fine one day can be pulled up with one hand the next because all of their roots have been eaten. Voles are to gardens as terrorists are to nation states.

So you probably don't want to know how cute they are. About 3 inches long, the pine vole has soft brown fur on the upper two-thirds of his body, slicker gray fur on the lower third. Although it can look more rat-like (i.e., less cute) stretched out, a pine vole cowering in the bed of a wheelbarrow is a round, little fluffy thing. He has a short tail, less than an inch long, broadish nose, small eyes, and barely-there ears. His blunt head makes him look even less rat-like than a meadow vole. Pine voles are a bit smaller than meadow voles, have shorter tails, and spend nearly all their lives in extensive underground tunnels, unlike meadow voles which have both surface runways and underground tunnels.

In your hand, the pulsating part of the pine vole's body feels about as big as an olive, and this creature that I've cursed as a fiend shudders at the click of a camera.

It's hard to move on to telling you how to kill voles, but that is what I've resorted to after finding myself unable to control them. One can reduce vole damage in a variety of ways: keeping mulch away from the base of trees, protecting young seedlings and trees with plastic or hardware cloth cylinders, putting sharp crushed gravel in holes with bulbs, planting bulbs in screen cages, cultivating the soil to destroy burrows and reduce cover, using composted sewage sludge, which voles dislike the smell of, as fertilizer, and surrounding crops like potatoes with underground "fences" of hardware cloth. I had done most of that but still had a serious problem, because one can't barricade an entire garden, and one can't regularly cultivate a perennial bed. When my lawn became so riddled with runs that walking on it felt like walking on a water bed, I reluctantly put pelleted poison (zinc phosphide) in their tunnels. I may have killed some voles, but I lost my nerve, for fear of killing something other than a vole, before really controlling them.

What I haven't tried yet but may soon is what is now being recommended for lawn and garden vole control by the Extension Service—trapping with standard mouse traps. For pine voles, the traps, baited with apples, are placed perpendicular to the line of the tunnel in an area that has been excavated to allow the trap to rest flush with the bottom of the tunnel. Then the trap is covered with a curving piece of cardboard or roofing shingle. According to Extension Service publication No. 420-024, the whole area harboring voles should be trapped using at least one trap per 100 square feet, and if you'll do that, "After a week of trapping, the number of voles caught per day should be near zero." The mere thought of it is bliss!

Imagine my surprise, then, when my husband asked if I wanted him to release our pine vole from the wheelbarrow, and I heard myself answer "Yes."

In trying to explain that answer to myself, all I could think of were scenes from movies in which leaders of opposing forces greet each other on the battlefield, acknowledge each other as worthy opponents, then turn back to their troops and do what they have to do.

I had experienced a temporary truce with a vole, but war would resume the next day. In fact, the next day I found a

3-foot holly sapling lying on its side, went to straighten it, and discovered it had no roots. That rat!

Much Ado about Moss

After you have glutted your senses with the brilliant hues of flowers, mosses are both rest and refreshment, like a salad after curry.
— CHRISTOPHER LLOYD

To enjoy moss or to get rid of it; that is the question. Those of you who think it's nobler to get rid of it, hang on; I'm going to tell you how to get rid of it. But first, let me explain why you might want to keep it.

Too often we assume moss is to lawns as mold is to refrigerators. But a growing number of gardeners are beginning to appreciate moss as a groundcover. In Ashland, a home on College Avenue has a front lawn consisting almost entirely of moss and bluets. In the spring, walkers go out of their way to see it, but when the house was recently sold, we moss-lovers shuddered to think ChemLawn types might move in. We needn't have worried; the purchasers were soon seen weeding the grass out of the moss. Although heavy foot traffic will wear it down, moss provides an expanse of green that requires no mowing or chemical fertilizers. Whenever somebody asks me what to do about a spot where only moss will grow, I want to answer, "Why not grow moss?"

Moss is not a no maintenance groundcover, however. Weeds do grow in it, and occasionally, due to foot traffic or winter damage, it needs to be rejuvenated. Believe it or not, here is the recommended treatment for winter-damaged moss: a solution of one part buttermilk to seven parts water applied twice a day for two weeks. The buttermilk helps acidify the soil. Some experts also recommend fertilizing moss with manure tea, a solution made by "steeping" a porous bag of manure in water until the water takes on the color of weak tea.

There is also a way to get moss started in areas that have none by using a "moss starter." Because moss reproduces from stem pieces as well as from spores, a concoction that includes moss pieces can be spread on bare earth (or on wooden fences, shake shingles, rocks) to get moss started. To make moss starter, mix a handful of moss, a can of beer (or an equal amount of buttermilk), and ½ teaspoon sugar in a blender until a thick puree forms. Reportedly, spreading this mixture about ¼ inch thick on bare earth will result in moss in about five weeks. According to *Horticulture*'s Elsie Cox, you can also wrap wet bricks in cheesecloth, spread this mixture on the cheesecloth, wait for moss to form, then take the cheesecloth off and spread it on the ground. The cheesecloth will rot away, the moss remain.

You can also move moss from one part of the yard to another. Landscape designer Cynthia Gillis, who has experimented with using moss as a groundcover, says it transplants best if it's taken up when wet with rain, sprayed underneath with water, and moved to a site cleared of existing vegetation that has been made muddy by watering. Moisture it does need, and Gillis suggests burying a soaker hose under it and adding water absorbent crystals, such as Terra-Sorb, to the soil, although this begins to sound as labor-intensive as turf-building to me. I would say if your site is too dry to grow moss, don't grow moss.

To get rid of moss, do the opposite of everything I've recommended for growing it. Seriously, if you have moss growing in areas where you don't want it, you must first remove the growing conditions that moss likes. Prune trees to increase light and airflow, improve drainage, rake leaves, fertilize based on a soil test, aerate the soil, and mow frequently. Some experts recommend applying iron sulfate (3 ounces per 5 gallons of water per 1000 square feet) or copper sulfate (3 to 5 ounces per 5 gallons of water per 100 square feet) in the spring or applying 10 pounds of lime per 1000 square feet to kill moss.

It is easier by far to let it be.

Start Garden Jobs Small— They Grow Fast

Nothing grows faster than a garden job. Garden jobs send out runners like ajuga, and one job is attached to fifteen others before you know it. The only way I have found to handle this predicament is to give garden jobs plenty of room to spread. If you have a job that should take 15 minutes, plan to give it all afternoon.

Case in point. I decide to mow the side yard. By all rights, this should take 15 minutes since our side yard is no bigger than a bowling alley lane. But here is what happens.

Before I mow, I decide I should pull some of the grass away from the liriope. Otherwise, I'll be mowing down some of the liriope. The liriope, I discover, has spread too close to the fence. That's where I had wanted daffodils. I dig out the unwanted liriope which now needs a home. I decide to extend the established liriope bed to the left. This will require digging up some of the best grass in the yard. I decide to save the sod. This requires a bucket. The bucket is filled with sand. The sand could go in the coal scuttle. The coal scuttle is filled with wood ashes. To get a place to put the sand so that I'll have the bucket I need for the sod, I have to get rid of the wood ashes, so I decide to fertilize the lilacs. This means weeding around the lilacs before I spread the wood ashes.

When the sod finally makes it into the bucket, it needs watering. This requires untangling the hose. The hose is in a Gordian knot. To avoid dealing with the knot, I unscrew the hose and water the bucket of sod from the spigot.

Finally, I head to the part of the yard that will receive the sod. The bare spots need scratching up with a rake. The rake is nowhere to be found. Finding the rake requires straightening up the shed.

Finally, the sod gets plopped down onto the bare spots, but it won't have a chance without being watered in. Back to the hose and the Gordian knot.

Then there's the liriope still waiting to be planted where the sod was, and the compost that really should be added to the soil, and all the debris that now needs to be raked up. Before you know it, I'm two hours into mowing the side yard, and I still haven't started the lawn mower.

As I said, nothing grows faster than garden jobs. Be sure to give them plenty of room.

Plant Trees— Don't Bury Them

"That's quite a hole," I couldn't help commenting to the groundsman planting a tree at the Virginia Institute of Marine Science in Gloucester. The hole was about 5 feet deep, 4 feet wide, and 6 feet long.

"I've had a lot of practice," answered the groundsman. "I used to be a grave digger."

"Is that the tree you're going to plant?" I asked, pointing to a Bradford pear with a root ball about 2½ feet in diameter.

"Yep."

What I wanted to say next was "that hole is entirely too deep," but this is not a comment a lady passerby makes casually to a man who has spent all day digging a hole. Instead, I asked, "Does it need a hole that deep?"

"Yep," said the groundsman. "If you don't plant 'em deep they blow over."

Should I have argued? I didn't think so, even as I saw the Bradford pear lowered into its grave.

Conventional wisdom about tree planting is so deeply rooted it's almost impossible to grub out, but new research suggests many of our old ideas about trees and tree planting are wrong.

For example, most of us still harbor an image of tree roots going, if not to China, at least way into the bowels of the earth. In truth, most tree roots are within the top 18 inches of soil.

Many of us were also taught to believe that tree roots extended roughly to the tree's drip line (the edge of its canopy), but a healthy tree's root system often extends into an area one and a half to three times the diameter of its drip line.

All this has implications for the way we plant trees. For example, a wide hole is more important than a deep hole, and shallow planting is actually better for most trees than deep planting. The hole should be deep enough to allow the tree to grow at the same depth at which it grew at the nursery or a little higher, and all the ground preparation you need to do under the root ball is break up the soil a bit with your shovel. In heavy clay soils which drain poorly, nurserymen recommend "planting proud" which means planting the tree so that the root ball is a few inches above the ground level. Then you mound soil up around the root ball to the previous soil line.

There is some disagreement about how wide the hole should be. A hole twice to three times as wide as the root ball is still recommended by most experts, but I'm beginning to hear suggestions that the hole need be only slightly wider than the spread of the tree's roots. I'm still digging holes wider myself.

What nearly everyone seems to agree on these days, although it is at odds with what most of us were taught, is that we should do nothing to enrich the soil going back into the hole at planting time. No peat moss, no fertilizer, *nothing*. Research suggests that all we are doing by improving the soil that goes into a tree's planting hole is creating a flowerpot effect. That is, we are creating a zone of improved soil that the tree's roots won't want to grow out of instead of encouraging the roots' entry into the surrounding soil. In short, we are now being told not to coddle our roots; they need to get out into the real world as soon as possible. Scoring the sides and bottom of the planting hole with a spade, shovel, or mattock is important, because it breaks up slick sides of the hole—the sides of the flowerpot— and improves both aeration and root penetration.

According to tree guru Alex Shigo, fertilizing a tree at

planting time may encourage growth that the tree can't support. Shigo recommends waiting until the new tree has completed at least one growth cycle before fertilizing.

Where we should fertilize and water may also surprise you. Except for thoroughly soaking the entire planting area several times after planting, landscaper Robert Kourik says we should keep both fertilizers and water away from the trunk area to lure roots out into the peripheral soil. That means applying water and fertilizer just beyond the planting hole to encourage roots to reach for the water and nutrients. Kourik maintains that continual watering up close to the trunk will discourage roots from spreading and leave them vulnerable to drought.

One last word on planting trees has to do with the size tree to plant. Start small; it almost always pays off in the long run. Small trees are easier to establish than large ones, and they will often catch up with the larger ones. I once read about a nurseryman who planted two groups of cypress trees on the same property. Half of them were in 1-gallon pots and cost $4.95 each; the other half were in 15-gallon pots and cost $65 each. After four years, the 1-gallon trees were taller and sturdier than half of the 15-gallon trees. In *The International Book of Trees*, Hugh Johnson reports similar, if less dramatic, results, he says that in ten to fifteen years, a tree planted at half the height of a larger one will have raced ahead.

All this seems to suggest that tree planting may not be half as much work as we would like it to be. After all, if we can't prove how much we want our trees to succeed by digging gargantuan holes, pouring on lots of fertilizer, or buying the biggest tree on the lot, how can we prove it? Just leaving them alone, trying not to run over them with the lawn mover, and not replacing them with something else before they have a chance to get established will help, but in the end it's up to the tree. "It does them no good to try to make things easy for them," someone told me once about raising children. I guess the same thing holds true for trees.

April

Cowslips Earn Interest

I have just given away my one thousand three hundred and eleventh cowslip and am still feeling sad that there are others in the yard that need dividing, but I haven't the energy to divide them. This feels like having money sitting around under a mattress when it could be in a bank collecting interest, but there is a limit to the amount of investment banking a gardener can do.

I've been dividing cowslips since the days when my neighbor Bernice Levin gave me my first clump. Compact plants with crinkly bright green leaves and pale yellow flowers rising on 6- to 8-inch downy stems, cowslips invariably attract attention, especially from people familiar with prized English cowslips. What I have, I think, is a natural hybrid between the "real" English cowslip, *Primula veris*, and the English primrose, *Primula vulgaris*. My flowers aren't fragrant and aren't dominated by puffy calyxes the way real English cowslips are, but they are held in loose umbels (a candelabra-like arrangement) as English cowslips are but as English primroses, which usually have solitary flowers, are not. In my neighborhood, we call what I have cowslips and leave it at that.

Some Englishwomen nearly swoon in the presence of my cowslips, so reminiscent are they of English woodlands, but Virginia gardeners appreciate them no less. Not only is the cowslip a lovely, early spring perennial, it persists in the garden better than any other primrose I have ever grown. "Firstling of spring" is what *Primula veris* means, and this cowslip deserves that description. Not that it signals the arrival of warm weather, mind you. "God gave the primrose its rough leaves to hide it from the blast of an uneven spring," reads an entry on one of my calendars, and its author, G. MacDonald, knew both his primroses and his springs. March snows often bury the cowslip's bright green rosettes of crinkled leaves, but not only do they survive to bloom in April, they come through looking as though they've had nothing more than a good watering.

What cowslips suffer from more than cold are heat, drought, and humidity. In short, they would rather be in an English woodland than a Virginia garden, but that doesn't mean they will sulk. Given the right conditions—rich, moist, organic soil and bright shade—they will thrive and multiply. They are actually pretty adaptable, and you can move them around until you find a spot where they are happy. I grow cowslips on the north side of the house where it's shady and in a sunnier border where I sometimes have to provide them extra water. I also grow them on the steep banks along a Buckingham county stream, and it's there that they really seem most at home. I have read that cowslips particularly appreciate moisture in the spring while they are actively growing, but that, like many early spring wildflowers, they can do with less water later in the season, after active growth stops. Their foliage often withers away to nothing in the summer.

For a long time, I scattered cowslips around like greeting cards, hoping to plant a "welcome spring" message in every part of the yard where they'd grow, but I'm learning to pull flowers that bloom at the same time together so they can make one dramatic statement. In early spring, cowslips look great growing near *Iris reticulata* because the cowslip foliage looks fresh and green when these diminutive irises bloom. Virginia bluebells are also good companions for cowslips because they bloom at the same time and enjoy the same woodland conditions. So are 'Pipit' daffodils, which have that same chalky yellow color. 'Pink Panda' ornamental strawberries also make great companions for cowslips if you can find a spot where the cowslips will get enough shade, or supplemental water, and the Pink Pandas enough sun to coexist.

The only thing labor-intensive about growing cowslips is dividing them, and they do need frequent division because they multiply rapidly, forming tighter and tighter clumps. They should be divided after they bloom by teasing the crown apart and planting the offspring in soil enriched with organic matter; the organic mater will both resupply nutrients and help hold moisture. Make sure plenty of these new plants wind up in your own garden or neighborhood, because there is something you'll want to make that requires zillions of cowslip flowers.

It's a cowslip ball, and I learned how to make it from Gertrude Jekyll's *Children and Gardens*. After reading Jekyll's book, I found myself some children and went out to make this ball constructed of cowslip blooms. It's made by having two children (I suppose adults could do this, but they wouldn't look half so cute) hold a staunch thread or string between them while a third hangs cowslip flowers over it. The thread slips between flowers in the umbel. Then, the thread is gathered up until the flowers bunch together forming a tight ball, and the string is tied together in a knot. The result is sort of a floral Koosh ball that is as much fun to toss as it is to make.

"Why are they called cowslips?" the first pint-sized cowslip-ball maker I played with asked me, and I had to admit I didn't know the answer to this obvious question. Now I do: the word comes from the Old English *cu-slyppe*, which literally means cow dung, and harks back to the days when cowslips bloomed in pastures where dairy cows grazed.

Ancient lore surrounding cowslips includes medicinal and culinary uses, too. It has been suggested that one reason cowslips are relatively scarce now in English woodlands is that they were once collected by the gallons to make wine and to use in recipes that required enormous quantities of them. Recipes for pickles, cakes, syrups, creams, puddings, tarts, cheeses, and vinegars included cowslips. Herbalists also used cowslips in concoctions for treating "all diseases of the sinews" as well as for restoring beauty. The seventeenth-century English herbalist, Nicholas Culpeper, wrote "An ointment made with them (the flowers) taketh away spots and wrinkles of the skin, sun burnings and freckles and adds beauty exceedingly."

So where does one line up for these miraculous flowers? It used to be that it was difficult to find them for sale, but now many nurseries carry them. Local plant sales and garden club exchanges are other good sources, and, of course, any gardener who has them will certainly share. I give them to nearly every gardener who comes to my garden trolling for plants, sometimes explaining they're English cowslips, sometimes just saying "they'll grow."

Sorry, Kate, Most Plants Have a Brown Stage

As the first wave of daffodils fades leaving brown tissue paper blobs where yellow blossoms had been, I am reminded that most every plant has a "down stage" that we have either to endure or to cover up in the garden. Spent daffodil flowers can be picked off, an act that's helpful to the bulb but too much trouble if you have lots of daffodils, and yellowing daffodil foliage can be hidden by plants like peonies whose foliage is coming up as the daffodils are dying down. But for flowers like those of a white azalea which seem to go from perfect purity to perfect hideousness overnight, there's nothing to do save endure them and hope a hard rain speeds their demise. Even American hollies which seem permanently garbed in evergreen perfection have a period in mid-May when their old leaves turn yellow and hang on like damaged fingernails before they fall.

That most novice gardeners are unaware that plants have "down stages" and are distressed to discover them was brought home to me last month when my daughter bought the Ortho book of *Shade Gardening* and began her first love affair with a plant. The plant was Bishop's hat, found on page 81. At first I didn't recognize the name, but when Kate showed me the picture, I said, "Oh, that's epimedium. Wonderful plant. Great choice, one of my favorites, you'll love it." In spite of that, Kate still wanted it, which is the difference between a child over twenty and a teenager.

Then, in mid-March, Kate came to my house after work one night, and we went out back with a flashlight to look at my epimedium.

"That?" she gasped in horror.

In mid-March, especially after a hard winter, epimedium is a tangled mass of haywire stalks topped with dry brown leaves, the antithesis of the illustration on page 81 of the Ortho book, which shows dainty white flowers with purple spurs and lush green foliage.

Kate's reaction was immediate: "I don't want anything that has a brown stage."

Ah, to be twenty-something and believe there is anything without a brown stage! On second thought, maybe it's better to be middle aged and aware that nothing in the visible or invisible universe lacks a brown stage.

Now it is the beginning of April, and you should see the epimedium. The day after Kate left, I went out and brushed my hand through those desiccated brown leaves. That was all it took to make them drop to the ground and virtually disappear. Then the blooms came—delicate, arching 12-inch wands of tiny pale yellow flowers that look a little like strings of miniature columbine flowers. New leaflets are beginning to appear, too. They are heart-shaped, and their color is a beautiful olive green brushed with maroon.

My expanse of epimedium, which I'm mighty proud of, having divided the plants every year for seven years to make them spread, is gorgeous right now as clouds of yellow blooms float above the tiny verdigris leaves. When the leaves have completely unfurled, they'll cover the flowers, but by then it's this plant's handsome foliage I'll be praising.

I could go on about the virtues of epimedium. It grows in dry shade, and the foot-tall plants make an excellent groundcover. The plant's foliage, compound leaves that mature to a uniform light green, is wonderful to use in arrangements, as are the dainty flowers. It comes in many shapes and sizes, some more or less evergreen, and some with white, pinkish, purple, or yellow flowers. Its highest and best use is as a groundcover under a tree where nothing else will grow. There, its foliage will look handsome all spring, summer, fall, and most of the winter. What a shame I had to show mine to Kate in mid-March.

Enjoy Star of Bethlehem from Afar

Star of Bethlehem was as much a part of turn-of-the-century backyards as white sheets flapping on the line. In fact, the best description I ever heard of star of Bethlehem was from a neighbor who had just spotted a huge expanse of it blooming in Pearl Mitchell's backyard: "I thought a sheet had fallen off the line," she said.

The botanical name of this little European bulb is *Ornithogalum umbellatum*. It's a plant about 6 to 12 inches tall with flat, grassy, white-ribbed leaves that form tufts in the grass and in the garden. The 1-inch flowers that stand above this foliage are white on the inside and green on the outside. Each has six petals arranged like the points of a star (hence, the flower's name), and the individual flowers occur in candelabra-like clusters of five to twenty. The bulbs multiply rapidly, and the plant must also spread by seeds because it's famous for hopping all over the yard and has naturalized in many parts of the country.

One hesitates to call such an appealing little plant a weed, but here is what garden writer Eleanor Perenyi says about star of Bethlehem in *Green Thoughts*: "my worst lawn enemy doesn't appear on weed lists. Star of Bethlehem (*Ornithogalum umbellatum*) is a pretty little item in bulb catalogues, who sometimes offer it as a bonus on a large order. Don't touch it. It will invade every part of the garden, choking out everything in its path, and like many undesirables is cunningly constructed to thwart easy extraction—the slippery foliage when tugged instantly separates from the bulblets, leaving them snugly far below ground."

There's another reason for not growing star of Bethlehem, too: it is poisonous. Although all parts of the plant are poisonous, the bulb is particularly toxic and can cause cardiac problems if ingested. Now that I'm aware of star of Bethlehem's toxicity, the flower's faint fragrance, which used to remind me of lying in the grass and flying kites, now makes me think of skulls and crossbones.

So, should we plant star of Bethlehem or not? In gardens where children might graze or in gardens where the gardener wants complete control, the answer is clearly *no*. In a more naturalistic setting, maybe, although even there the gardener would be safer scratching his itch for starry white flowers by growing a better-behaved plant like *Phlox stolonifera* 'Bruce's White,' a beautiful groundcover that blooms a bit later. Windflowers (*Anemone blanda*) and candytuft (*Iberis sempervirens*) will also form sheets of white without blanketing the entire yard.

In my garden, I have two clumps of star of Bethlehem that I did not plant. I think they rode in on the roots of a spiderwort somebody gave me. Although I'm aware these handkerchief-sized clumps of white flowers could turn into king-sized sheets overnight, I still I haven't tried to grub them out, because they communicate an old-fashioned charm I like. On the other hand, what I would really like is to be able to get rid of my star of Bethlehem secure in the knowledge there will always be a Pearl Mitchell's yard nearby where I can enjoy these white flowers from afar, because beautiful as star of Bethlehem is, it is best loved in someone else's yard.

Fire Pink Ignites Arrangements

It is such a serious offense to pick rare wildflowers that conservationists are loath to mention it when a native plant makes a great cut flower. Even prolific wildflowers often suffer from over-collection, but for the arranger who is willing to grow his or her own cut flowers, there are some native plants an arranger's garden shouldn't be without.

Fire pink, *Silene virginica*, is my favorite wildflower for cutting. In the wild, where the fiery red blooms of a single fire pink can light up a roadside, cutting a fire pink would be like defacing a national monument, but in my garden where I can monitor their reproduction, I can cut a few fire pink blossoms and still have plenty left to set seed. Because not all of the flowers on a fire pink plant produce fruit, "pick sparingly" is the rule even for backyard collectors, but it takes no more than a single stalk of fire pink to beautify a bud vase.

It's the color and shape of the fire pink's bloom that make it such a spectacle in the wild, in the garden, and in arrangements. A member of the Pink (*Caryophyllaceae*) Family, the fire pink has five narrow, fire engine red petals, each of them notched at the end. The flowers are about 1½- to 2-inches wide, and they bloom in loose clusters at the tops of slender 1- to 2-foot stems. These stems have a tendency to flop over in the garden, but in arrangements they stand as straight as flagpoles. In my garden, fire pinks are always blooming during Virginia's Historic Garden Week—the third week in April, and they continue blooming until the second or third week of May. On Thunder Ridge in Virginia's Blue Ridge Mountains, one naturalist recorded a colony of fire pinks blooming for an extraordinary eight weeks—from May 7 to July 7.

Dry open woods and rocky slopes from Ontario to Alabama are the habitats in which you are likely to find fire pinks, and you'll grow them best where you can provide them similar well-drained soils. The soil need not be rich; like columbines, they like thin soils. Fire pinks are not finicky about exposure either—they will grow in full sun or part shade, although the more sun you give them the less floppy their flower stalks will be. A spot along the woodland edge or in a sunny rock garden is ideal; mine bloom beautifully both in a raised bed under an elm and in a sunny garden bed. The most beautiful clump of them I ever saw in the wild bloomed at the edge of a low woodland with woodland phlox (*Phlox divaricata*).

Hardy in zones 3 through 8, fire pinks are usually described as short-lived perennials. I once took exception to this, arguing that I didn't think they were so short-lived since I had a plant that was 5 years old and Thurman Maness of North Carolina's Wildwood Nursery had a fire pink that had persisted in his garden for 10 years. Then my 5-year-old plant died. I've come to realize it is pretty common for fire pink's compact, 6- to 12-inch basal rosettes to die out after a couple of years, so I always try to have some new plants coming along. If you're really lucky, you will have self-sown seedings to replace your old plants, but you can also generate new plants by dividing old ones in early spring or late fall. Be aware that although fire pink's basal rosettes are evergreen, they shrink dramatically over the winter, so don't think you have lost them just because they're not prominent; they will stretch back to size in the spring.

Fire pinks have sticky stems and calyxes that trap small insects (members of the genus *Silene* are commonly called "Catch-flies"), but other than aphids which trouble *Silene* in the greenhouse, they are generally untroubled by insect pests. When fire pinks are mulched up to the base of the plants, slugs and rot can be problems, but I keep the ground around my plants free even of leaf litter.

Because they don't have strong root systems, fire pinks can't tolerate much competition, so choosing what to grow them with can be tricky. You can avoid the issue by growing them as solitary accents in rock gardens, or you can grow them with shy companions. In the partial shade under my elm, the companions I like best with my fire pinks are the diminutive star chickweed (*Stellaria pubera*) and rue anemone (*Anemonella thalictroides*). Both are nonaggressive native plants whose tiny white flowers provide a perfect foil to the dazzling red of the fire pinks. In arrangements, I also love to combine fire pinks with snow-in-summer (*Cerastium tomentosum*), and since snow-in-summer isn't as rampant in my garden as its reputation suggests it should be, I'm screwing up my courage to try growing the two plants together. A clump of *Silene virginica* surrounded by *Cerastium tomentosum* would be as spectacular as a bonfire on a snow bank.

Silene virginica is one of the few *Silene* species with stems long and strong enough to work as a cut flower, but there is a new introduction, a cross between *Silene virginica* and *Silene polypetala*, the Fringed Campion, I am eager to try. A low-growing *Silene* with pink flowers, *Silene polypetala* is a rare Georgia native that has being propagated from cuttings and tissue culture. The deep pink flowered *Silene virginica* × *polypetala* has the fringed petals of its Georgia parent, the greater vigor and longer stems of the fire pink. When I asked Longwood Gardens' Jim Ault, who helped develop the plant, if he thought its flowers might hold up after cutting, he said he thought they might. In fact, instead of fussing at me for cutting my *Silene* as I had feared he might, he said judicious flower harvesting may make the plants more vigorous. What music to the ears of the native plant enthusiast who also loves cut flowers!

Whichever Way It Winds, Wisteria Is Beautiful

Here's a question for you: does your wisteria wind clockwise or counterclockwise as it climbs? The answer is significant because if it winds counterclockwise, you have Chinese wisteria, if it winds clockwise, you have Japanese wisteria. No joke. I'm pretty sure I have Chinese wisteria, but it wasn't easy deciding which way the vine twines. A meeting under our vines last night led to a split decision. My daughter and I thought the vines were winding clockwise until my husband John came out and showed us— I guess—that we weren't following the direction of growth. "This is three o'clock, this is twelve o'clock, this is nine o'clock," John kept arguing as he pointed to the spiraling vine with his flashlight.

I might still be arguing that it depends on how you look at it, except for other evidence that ours is the Chinese wisteria. Chinese wisteria, *Wisteria sinensis*, is the more common of the two species, has flower clusters 6 to 12 inches long, and flowers all at once. Japanese wisteria, *W. floribunda*, has flower clusters 8 to 20 inches long and blooms over a longer period of time. The only evidence that has me confused is that Japanese wisteria is supposed to be more fragrant than Chinese wisteria, and I can't imagine flowers more fragrant than ours.

There is something so cloyingly sweet about wisteria blossoms that where the vines have been allowed to run rampant, you could swoon in the heavy-scented air. Bees love the blossoms, and it would be dangerous to sit on our front porch on a warm day if the wisteria flowers weren't so much more attractive to the bees than we are.

There are only three problems with growing wisteria: it sometimes takes forever to bloom, it is often nipped in the bud by frost, and it takes a gardener with the temperament of Rambo to keep it in check.

Rampant growth is wisteria's most famous drawback. "It will pull the house down," I've been told more than once, and I believe it. I've watched those twining shoots reach out and grab my rocking chairs on the front porch, and our porch columns still bear the scars where the vines wrapped around the wood and began to squeeze it as they grew. It will grow up under shingles, pull down gutters, and in one famous case, it grew right under the siding of a house and straight into a lady's bedroom. Imagine a canopy of wisteria hanging over the bed!

Still, I grow it on the house, which means I am locked in battle with it all the time. I don't let it wrap around anything, which is like trying to keep teenage lovers apart. When I saw what it was doing to the columns, I pulled it down and made it start all over again. As it grew up, I led it up along the columns and screwed big hooks into the woodwork along the porch. These hooks, not the twining of the vines, are to hold it up. Over and over I repeat this to the wisteria; over and over the wisteria makes straightaway for the gutters.

I am forever cutting it back and pulling it down. The experts say to prune established plants heavily after they flower and again in winter. They recommend cutting out all weak wood and trimming new shoots to within six buds from the base of the branch. I cut mine back whenever it's reaching for something it is not supposed to have. And I am planning to replace those big hooks, which the wisteria is already outgrowing, with heavier wooden supports that will support the main vines like shelf brackets.

Wisteria seedlings will pop up all over the yard, and I have shared these with friends for whom they've grown and bloomed, but this may not be the best way of acquiring plants. Wisteria seedlings can be hard to dig out, and sometimes they won't bloom for a decade after being moved. Experts say it's better to buy blooming plants from a nursery, where you can usually purchase them for under $20. They grow best in full sun with some protection from the wind, and although some nurserymen recommend a high phosphorus fertilizer like bone meal or superphosphate for wisteria, I've never fertilized mine.

Most wisterias, of which there are nine or ten species, have blue, lilac, or white flowers, but some have pink flowers. The flowers can also vary in size. I read once that a Japanese wisteria flower cluster measured in this country was 36 inches long and that a specimen grown in Japan had a flower cluster 64 inches long! There is also a wisteria native to the southeast. This wisteria, *Wisteria frutescens*, has shorter racemes of flowers than either Chinese or Japanese wisteria, and if I were to start over with wisteria, this is the one I would grow. I've seen this lavender-flowered wisteria growing both on the edge of moist, fertile woods near Ashland and on fences in Colonial Williamsburg, and not only is it a lovely vine, it is less aggressive than exotic wisterias.

In addition to beautiful flowers, wisteria has attractive pods. They are about as long as pea pods and have a velvety exterior. I like to add them to dried wreaths, but beware: they'll twist open, projecting seeds across the room! I've tried to catch them in the act of opening but haven't succeeded. What usually happens is that I leave an unopened pod on my desk and come back to find the pod open and the flat, black seeds scattered on the floor.

There is half a pod still sitting on my desk right now, and it occurs to me that it must spiral the same way the vines do. If I follow the direction of the spiral from stem to tip, it seems to be spiraling in a counterclockwise (Chinese) direction. Amazing! How Chinese wisteria knows to go one way and Japanese wisteria knows to go the other I have no idea, but I keep rolling the pod around in my hand hoping the mystery will rub off on me.

When a Weed Is a Welcome Thing

Admittedly, adults are slow at these things, but when the faculty of a local high school went hunting for five hundred Easter eggs hidden on and around the football field, you would have thought they could find *some*. It wasn't until one of the hiders whispered "Pssst! Look in the wild onions" that baskets started filling up.

What masters of concealment these hiders were, because a wild onion can swallow an Easter egg the way a cat swallows a canary. All the hider has to do is wiggle the egg down under the onion's matted old foilage.

Onions aren't the only weeds hiding eggs around Easter. It is an unusual basket that doesn't hold an egg found in proximity to henbit or purple dead nettle, two of our most common spring weeds. Of the two, henbit (*Lamium amplexicaule*) is the more beautiful. Get down on you hands and knees and take a close look at its bright pinkish-purple flowers. Instead of typical petals, each flower has an upright "hood" topping a lower "lip." The mature ½- to ⅔-inch flowers emerge in whorls from scalloped leaves that clasp the stem in pairs. The plant's species name *amplexicaule*, in fact, means "clasping" or "embracing" and describes the way these horizontally held leaves hug the stem. Another identifying feature of henbit is the big spaces between the pairs of leaves on the plant's thin, square stems. Look for repeated sequences of two clasping leaves, then stem space, then leaves.

What I love most about henbit, however, is the color and configuration of its buds. These tiny (1/16- to 1/2-inch), velvety-textured drops of bright purple are so saturated with color they literally light up against the background of the nosegay-like leaves behind them. Thumbelina would have carried henbit buds at her wedding.

Purple dead nettle (*Lamium purpureum*) is a less refined, smaller plant (to 8 inches) than henbit, but when it's not crowding peony shoots or spreading a mat of fibrous roots across your garden, it has its own appeal. Its lavender, lipped flowers are borne in the leaf axils, and its heart-shaped leaves congregate near the top of the plant's square stems. Slightly furry and blunt-toothed, its 1/3- to 1-inch leaves are a dull green tinged with purple—the uppermost ones exhibit the most purple—which accounts for the "purple" in the plant's name. It is called dead nettle because it doesn't have the stinging bristles along its square stem that true nettles do.

Run your fingers up the stem of purple dead nettle and you will discover two things—the plant's fragrance, which to me brings back memories of Easters past, and its seeds, which spill out as you dislodge them. Watch to see if birds eat these seeds, because it seems they should. Henbit gets its name from the fact that chickens eat its seeds.

Both henbit and purple dead nettle are related to other members of the genus *Lamium* that we grow as ornamentals. *Lamium maculatum* 'Beacon Silver,' for example, is a popular ground cover. The British use the common name Archangel to refer to many members of the Lamium clan, presumably because they bloom around May 8, the feast day of the Archangel Michael.

Both henbit and purple dead nettle are annual weeds that most gardeners would wish away, but there is a bright side to their presence at Easter. You watch: when egg-hiders head out Easter morning, it won't be to the lawns rid of broadleaved weeds, and it won't be to lawns mowed specially for the occasion. The best lawns will be those of homeowners too poor or principled to use ChemLawn and too tardy taking their mowers in for spring tune-ups to have them back by Easter. On Easter morning, a weed is a welcome thing, if only to hide an egg.

May

Grow a Crop of Cornflowers

"Bachelor's buttons" is the name I usually use when referring to the bright blue wildflowers blooming along roadsides in May, but farmers call them "cornflowers," and it's farmers who, inadvertently, seem to grow them best. Wheatflowers is what they should be called because they seem to bloom best at the edges of wheat fields.

I'm particularly interested in the wheat-cornflower connection this year, because, after years of growing cornflowers with some success in the garden and with good success in a meadow, I now have the best crop of them I've ever had—in the lawn. Wheat straw, I've finally figured out, is the reason for this year's cornflower extravaganza, because the seeds rode in on wheat straw put down to hold grass seed in the fall. At first I thought the seeds might have been spread by goldfinches who fight me for the cornflower seeds each summer, then I thought they might have ridden in on new topsoil, but the real "culprit" became obvious when, in an unmowed area, the cornflowers started blooming among wheat stalks!

If this new lawn were in front of Buckingham Palace, the landscaper who spread straw with fresh wheat and "weed" seeds in it would probably have been sued, but in front of our Buckingham County cabin, we would have paid extra for these wildflowers in the grass. In fact, gardeners who want to grow cornflowers can take a lesson from this happy accident, because in terms of meeting the cornflower's cultural requirements, the man who spread our wheat straw did everything right.

First, he "planted" the seeds in the fall. Almost everything you read will tell you to start cornflower seeds indoors in late winter or to plant the seeds outdoors in early spring as soon as the ground can be worked. But all my "best" cornflowers have been planted in the fall. Some of them germinate before winter sets in; others come up in early spring. Although they are annuals, which sprout, mature, and die in a single year, cornflowers are hardy annuals that like to get their start in cool weather.

They don't resent transplanting as much as many other early-blooming annuals like larkspur and field poppies do, but they perform better and bloom earlier if planted as seeds where they are to grow.

How late in the season can you plant them and still get blooms this year? Good question. Until last year, I would have said you needed to get them up and blooming before hot weather set in, but that was before I'd seen a November crop. Last year around Thanksgiving I was shocked to walk out on my back porch and find a bucket of cornflowers a friend had left me. She'd picked them from around the perimeter of a field. I have asked the owner of that field to keep track of plowing dates to help me figure out when those cornflowers were "planted," but for now all I know is that, given a fall as mild as that of 1994, blooming cornflowers are possible in November. They make great cut flowers and even keep their intense blue color when dried.

As to where to plant them, again, take your cue from a wheat or corn field—they like full sun and well-drained soil. Plowing benefits them by "planting" the seeds and by keeping competing weeds down. When sowing them into a tilled garden area, watch carefully for the emerging silvery seedlings, because they are easy to confuse with weeds.

From mature plants, you can gather your own seeds. Seeds from cornflowers that have been reproducing in the wild for a while produce flowers with fewer petals and a more ragged look than flowers from store-bought seeds, but both are beautiful. About ¼ inch long, cornflower seeds are hard, almost nut-like, bristle-topped affairs, and you'll find them housed in the "base" of spent flowers. So fond are goldfinches of these seeds that I can almost promise you you'll have goldfinches if you have cornflowers. A friend with eyesight worse than mine once didn't believe me when I told her the spots of yellow she was seeing among the cornflowers that surround my vegetable garden were goldfinches; she insisted they were dandelions until we approached and the dandelions flew away!

Cornflowers are not native wildflowers; they were introduced from Europe but have naturalized here. I've read they were called Hurt Sickle in England, where farmers despised them, but when I asked a farmer in the Ashland Feed Store how cornflowers could "hurt a sickle," he gave me that "another-stupid-question-from-a-city-slicker look" and said, "I think somebody's pulling your leg."

Other common names for cornflowers (*Centaurea cyanus*) include ragged sailor, blue bottle, French pink, and my favorite, bachelor's buttons. One story about the origin of the bachelor's button name holds that the name came from the practice of English maidens wearing the flowers as signs that they were eligible for marriage. Another story holds that it came from the fact that bachelors, who couldn't sew on their own buttons, used these flowers, which have bulging, thistle-like bases, like cufflinks to hold their clothes together.

Whatever its source, the name "bachelor's buttons" suggests

a way I've always wanted to use the flowers—as boutonnieres in the lapels of eligible bachelors, maybe groomsmen at a May wedding. Certainly collecting them from a wheat field would beat paying a florist for carnations.

Gone Gardening

A handyman named Catfish helped teach me what it means to be hooked on gardening.

The day before Catfish was to come to hang sheetrock in my daughter's bedroom, our son pulled down all the plaster (no small task) and our daughter moved into the den (no small inconvenience). Two weeks later, Catfish still hadn't arrived. I should have been forewarned by the name, because Catfish, of course, had gone fishing.

At the time I wondered how anyone could be so irresponsible, but I'm beginning to identify with Catfish.

What I've discovered is, there are some things like fishing and gardening that just can't be planned to occur on schedule. How can one know when the fish will be biting or the soil ready to be tilled? How can a gardener predict in advance when the weeds will emerge or the sun insist she go digging? There are some days so auspicious for gardening (and, I suspect, for fishing) that to do anything else seems like a sacrilege.

The problem is, it's impossible to keep those perfect afternoons open for gardening without saying "no" ahead of time to everything that might interfere. "No," you would have to say to the friend asking you in January to help out with a PTA function in May, "I'm sorry, I'd love to help, but the weather might be pretty that afternoon." An equally unacceptable alternative is to say "yes" with conditions: "yes, I'd be happy to help as long as it's raining, snowing, or too cold to work outside."

The question that strikes greatest fear in a gardener's heart is "when will you be free?" because it threatens every afternoon you've been protecting for gardening. Can you say you're busy if you are merely hoping to garden—and then not feel like a truant when the person who asked if you were free rides by and sees you in the garden with a hoe in your hand?

There are some things, I know, that take precedence over gardening. Making a living and attending your children's weddings are nonnegotiable. But it's the optional stuff that feels most oppressive when it crowds a good gardening day. "Why am I here?" I've wondered as I stood around many a punch bowl. "How did I get into this?" I have wondered as I attended many a lecture while Spring 101 was going on outside.

Because of his passion for irises, the infinitely wise garden columnist Henry Mitchell suggested declining every human contact that could possibly be declined during the short time they are in bloom. But not everyone shares such a passion, and therein lies the rub. To most people gardening is what you do when there are no good sports on TV, when the shrubs need trimming, or when your spouse demands help with yardwork. How can we make them understand that for some of us, gardening is an imperative? We need it as much as we need water; we take our strength from the sun on our backs and our inspiration from watching things grow.

I see two possible solutions. One is to raise the status of gardening. No more of this hobby stuff. Let's raise gardening to the status of motherhood. No one has ever questioned my missing work, a meeting, or a social function in order to minister to the needs of a child. What I would like is similar dispensation for the days I'm called to nurture the earth.

Short of that, I'll have to take my cue from Catfish and adopt an appropriate nickname. Just call me Rosie or Buttercup, and know that my garden comes first.

Lily of the Valley: Delicate but Indestructible

Tired of ivy, bored with pachysandra? How about using lily of the valley as a ground cover for shady areas? I wish I could spirit all of you over to the north side of Cecil and Jim Cox's house and show you the carpet of lily of the valley there. Uninterrupted lily of the valley spreads to cover an area about 15 feet wide and 50 feet long. In May, between each pair of smooth 6-inch-tall leaves rises an arching wand of fragrant, white, ¼-inch, bell-shaped flowers. "They're so sweet-smelling, we can smell them the minute we walk out on the front porch," says Cecil.

Flower arrangers who prize lily of the valley leaves and flowers for arrangements, would grow this beautiful plant even if they had to make a special place for it in the cutting garden, but, elegant as it looks, lily of the valley doesn't need special accommodations. It's happiest in moist, rich soil in semi-shade, but it will grow in full shade, although it flowers less well there, and, once established, it's remarkably long-lived. This is one of the perennials our grandmothers were effortlessly growing before anyone had ever coined the term "low-maintenance." In fact, lily of the valley (*Convallaria majalis*) has naturalized— moved out into the wild—in some Virginia counties.

There are only two drawbacks to using lily of the valley as a groundcover. The first is that you can't walk on it. "When the girls were young, they would love to swish through it," says Cecil. "They liked the sound the leaves made when they walked or ran or rode a bike through them." But the lily of the valley suffered from their activity. "We had to put up gates so they couldn't swish," says Cecil. But few groundcovers other than grass, camomile, and thyme can take foot traffic. Use lily of the valley where pedestrians don't go.

Lily of the valley's other drawback is that it disappears entirely in the winter. "It looks real bad," says Cecil of the area that's bare after the lily of the valley leaves turn a beautiful yellow then disappear in the fall. If a winter bare spot really bothers you, you can grow lily of the valley under evergreen pachysandra, periwinkle, or even English ivy. Lily of the valley has been coming up through old English ivy on the north and east sides of my house for the 18 years I've lived here and for who knows how long before that. That these fragile blossoms and smooth, flawless leaves have the ability to muscle their way through thick, coarse ivy never ceases to amaze me. It's like seeing a ballerina stand up to a brute.

I have never fertilized or watered my lilies of the valley and I've divided them only to share plants. Even with such little attention, they've bloomed beautifully. Experts recommend dividing them every three years, because when they get too crowded, they produce fewer flowers. The plants grow from "pips," little bud-like appendages on underground fleshy roots, and these can be separated and replanted in early spring or early fall. Once established, they spread quickly.

One expert I consulted said lily of the valley "enjoys a top-dressing in early spring of well-rotted manure or compost enhanced with a dash of fertilizer." Another said a bed of lily of the valley will respond to an application of well-rotted manure in the fall. The Coxes give their lily of the valley a little lime in the fall when they fertilize the grass. That's interesting because lily of the valley is said to prefer acid soil, and lime reduces acidity, but no one would quarrel with the Cox's success. What these different prescriptions for success suggest to me is that lily of the valley is nearly indestructible and will survive in spite of what we do for it.

Prune after Flowering (Or When the Knife Is Sharp)

Little did John Shalf know when he chopped down his mother's favorite flowering shrub to make room to work on his jalopy, that he was doing the shrub a favor. Certainly his mother, coming upon a circle of 6-inch stubs where her 8-foot *Kerria japonica* 'Pleniflora' had been, was not amused.

"I was furious with him," said Ashlander Rosanne Shalf.

But that was six years ago. Now John has driven off to Illinois in his 1977 Volkswagen bus, and his mom is reaching to the top of said shrub on a ladder.

What John Shalf had done, albeit unwittingly, is what we should all be doing—pruning a spring-flowering shrub after blooming. Granted, he got a little radical, but even at that he was pruning by the book. "Multiple stem shrubs which have been neglected and have become quite dense may be cut down to short stubs for renewal," says a Virginia Tech publication.

The first and easiest rule of pruning to remember is "prune after flowering." Experts at the American Horticultural Society go so far as to extend this rule to spring-, summer-, and fall-flowering shrubs, noting that if you follow it, you will never have to worry about cutting off the next year's flowers. Pruning after flowering removes old flower buds, allowing the shrub to use its energy to make new ones.

The beauty of the "prune after flowering" rule is that you don't have to worry about knowing which shrubs bloom on new wood and which ones bloom on old wood—a distinction some gardeners can't make. The problem with the rule is that there are exceptions; some summer- and fall-blooming shrubs, for example, are better off being pruned in late winter or very early spring, rather than being pruned immediately after flowering. But forget about those for now; you need to be pruning your spring-blooming shrubs that have finished flowering—shrubs like andromeda, azalea, deutzia, forsythia, Japanese quince, kerria, lilac, pearlbush, and spirea.

Or, I should say, you need to be pruning them if they need pruning. Don't think you need to prune just because everyone else is doing it. The reasons for pruning are to improve a plant's health or appearance; if yours are healthy and a size and shape you like, leave them alone.

Prune if they've gotten too big, ragged, or dense, or if they have dead or diseased wood that needs to be removed.

In addition to the pruning we do for shape, which is usually all young shrubs need, mature, multistemmed shrubs like spirea and forsythia often need thinning "from the inside" to keep them full and vigorous. Cutting out some of the oldest stems at the base of the shrub each year stimulates interior growth, allows light and air to enter, and keeps the shrub "young at heart."

The advice "cut a few of the oldest stems at the base each year" sounds easy, but the reality of finding yourself under a 20-year-old spirea looking for the oldest canes can be daunting. How do you know which stems are the oldest? They're usually stiffer, woodier, and thicker than the newer ones, but don't despair if you're not 100 percent sure you're cutting the right ones. You can't make too big a mistake if you're only taking out a few each year.

Most pruning fears are way overblown. Light pruning can be done almost any time of year without seriously weakening a shrub, and many a successful gardener would admit she prunes whenever she feels like it (of course, experienced gardeners often "feel like it" at the correct time). Even Liberty Hyde Bailey, the father of American horticulture, suggested timing was less important than a clean cut. "Prune when the knife is sharp," he said. So keep your tools sharp for whoever happens to use them.

Don't Banish Buttercups

"If it's dry enough, I'm going to mow," my husband announced before heading off to our cabin in the mountains. Some wives would have celebrated, but not his.

Please don't mow the buttercups," I pleaded. Saving the buttercups was important because Sunday was Mother's Day, my mother would be visiting, and she and I share "a thing" about buttercups. The year I learned buttercups were perennial, we transplanted buttercups into the garden together, and ever since, we've considered it our "connection flower."

"All mothers love buttercups," a friend once told me. "It's because so many children pick them for Mother's Day bouquets." I can't remember having done that, but I do know I've always shared my mother's love for this simple flower.

There is really only a short period in May when the buttercups are at their peak—right around Mother's Day. Unfortunately, that is when the grass always seems to need cutting, and most people's buttercups are in the grass. You can mow buttercups down at least once in April and still get blooms for Mother's Day, however. And what blooms they are! The petals' shiny yellow color is as straightforward as children, their texture as smooth as silk. Even the buttercup's deeply cut leaves are decorative. In a one-on-one beauty contest with a rose, all other things being equal, a buttercup would win as often as it would lose.

Unfortunately, as people are forever pointing out to me, all other things aren't equal. Buttercups share the problem inherent in all things weedy: they're common. Their other liabilities are that they are slightly poisonous if ingested, and they have a substance in their roots that reportedly stunts the growth of neighboring plants. An acrid juice in their stems and leaves has been known to blister skin, although it's never blistered mine, and beggars are said to have used buttercup juice to produce ulcerations in the skin to attract sympathy. According to folklore, smelling too many of them will drive you crazy.

Maybe that's why I'm so crazy about buttercups.

I should admit, however, that as much as I enjoy buttercups in my own grass, the place I like them best is in other people's meadows where I don't have to worry about the speed with which they spread. In fact, in other people's meadows, abundance is one of the buttercup's chief assets. Ever see a field of them you thought was too yellow? And what child ever despaired over having too many buttercups to choose from when making a necklace of them? If you have never done this, slip the blossom of one buttercup into a slit you've made in the stem of another until you've made a chain long enough to slip over your head.

Ranunculus bulbosus is the botanical name of the buttercup in my grass and in most of the meadows near my house. It's identified by the bulbous swelling above its feeder roots and by the way its sepals, the modified leaves under the petals, point straight down. *Ranunculus acris*, known for its acrid stems and leaves, is another common buttercup. The genus name *Ranunculus* means "little frog" in Latin and reportedly refers to the preference of many plants in this genus for moist sites. Native to Europe but naturalized here, buttercups actually come in many different shapes and sizes. There are buttercups called kidney-leaf buttercups, creeping buttercups, and swamp buttercups. Now and then there are also individual plants of common buttercups that take unusual forms. I once found a mutant buttercup with flat stems over an inch wide and flowers that looked like two or three fused together.

The shiny, reflective surface of buttercup flowers is another unusual feature of the plants. I have a book that tells me this waxy texture is caused by a special layer of cells just beneath the surface cells. Botanists may disagree, but I'm sure this "special layer of cells" evolved to give the buttercup the reflectivity necessary to do what we all know buttercups were created to do: that is, to tell us who likes butter and who doesn't. Predating the cholesterol check by centuries, buttercups have been revealing the butter-lovers among us this way every spring: put a buttercup under the chin of a friend and if he loves butter, the yellow of the flower will be reflected on his skin; if he doesn't, it won't.

How could anyone think of mowing all these fabulous flowers away? Well, if, like John, in addition to having your mother-in-law, who loves buttercups, coming for dinner, you have your own mother, who doesn't like grass around her ankles, coming, you might consider it. With his usual wisdom, however, John mowed a path to the front door for his mother, leaving the rest of the buttercups untouched. King Solomon could have done no better.

Mystery Plant Turns Out to Be Treasure

For all our fiddling with labels and garden notes to keep plants and plant names straight, the mystery plants are still often the most fun. "It's probably a weed," I have said to myself a thousand times on seeing the leaf of a seedling I've never seen before. "But what if it's not?" is my next thought, which is why I let it grow. A pigweed once grew to 6 feet before I had satisfied myself it was a weed, and I'm still battling daisy fleabane offspring from the year I let in an invasion of them just to see what they were.

But now and then comes a surprise that makes all the free rides you've given weed seeds seem worth it.

My latest surprise rode in on a clump of thimbleweed. Thimbleweed (*Anemone virginiana*) is a wonderful perennial wildflower with anemone-like white flowers, thimble-like seed head, and three-part, deeply cut leaves. A neighbor, Ann Gilman, had dug a clump of thimbleweed up for me from her garden in the fall, and this spring I was delighted to see the plant's leaves coming up. But what were those lance-shaped leaves beside them? Thinking they might be a different growth form of thimbleweed, I let both grow until it was clear I had two plants sharing the same spot. By mid-April the thimbleweed leaves were dwarfed by a towering 3-foot plant with a hairy stem and lance-shaped leaves. It looked a little like a garden phlox but was too early for that.

What could it be? Knowing the wealth of plant material in Ann Gilman's garden, the possibilities seemed endless.

By the end of April a dozen buds had appeared on the plant and by the beginning of May both the buds and I were about to pop.

Finally, my mystery plant bloomed, and it was more beautiful than anything I could have imagined. It looked like a garden phlox with loose terminal clusters of flowers in the lightest shade of lavender, and a fragrance so wonderful I made dozens of unnecessary trips across the lawn just to get a whiff of it. Strangely enough, some people I invited to smell my mystery flower couldn't smell it; others found the fragrance overpowering. But no one seemed to know what the plant was. I thought it must be a wild phlox until I realized the flowers had four petals instead of the phlox's five.

Dame's rocket (*Hesperis matronalis*) is what my mystery plant turned out to be. I found it in a field guide listed as a plant that originally came from Europe but escaped from gardens and found a home in the wild in the eastern United States. Not two weeks after I learned what it was, I saw it blooming along roadsides near Winchester, where it is both common and widely known.

It's a biennial, so I will have to make sure it reseeds in order to have new plants coming along. At least now I know what its seedlings look like, so I won't pull them out. Should Dame's Rocket continue to grow for me, it will always have a special status in my garden, and not just because it's a lovely wildflower but because it might have been a weed.

Close Encounters of the Toad Kind

"In the name of the Prophet, [send] Toads!" That's the emergency message nineteenth-century poet Celia Thaxter sent her friend on the New Hampshire mainland when her island garden was being devoured by slugs. Soon a package arrived in the mail bearing what Thaxter thought were only a couple of dry-looking toads until she poured cooling water on them and "the dry, baked earth heaved tumultuously." Up popped "dusky heads and shoulders and bright eyes by the dozen."

"You are not handsome," wrote Thaxter in her garden

notes, "but you will be lovely in my sight if you will help me destroy mine enemy." And they did.

Toads have always been dear to the hearts of gardeners, who know they make the best bug zappers. Fifty to a hundred bugs a night is reportedly about an average night's work for a toad, and although they eat earthworms, naturalist Mary Dickerson reports in *The Frog Book* that earthworms make up only about 1 percent of a toad's diet; 88 percent of it, she says, consists of bugs considered pests of the garden, grain field, or pasture. In addition to slugs, toads eat cutworms, squash bugs, tent caterpillars, gypsy moth larvae, sowbugs, weevils, and other injurious beetles.

I've tried to watch a toad friend of mine eat, but without success. Every afternoon Mr. Toad, looking fat, sassy, and ready for a cigar, takes up his position at the entrance to his hole under my porch at almost the same moment I take my position in the rocker above him. Toads hunt at night, sometimes hopping around in search of food, sometimes waiting for it to come to them. After the sun goes down, I've shined my flashlight on him trying to watch him catch bugs, but all I've seen so far is the stretching expansion and contraction of his elastic throat. His tongue must thrust in and out faster than I can see it in the dim light.

The best way to keep toads around is to provide them water, food (no problem there if your garden has bugs), and shelter. Unlike smooth-skinned frogs, which spend their lives in or near water, toads, their warty-skinned counterparts, leave the water after the tadpole stage and spend their adult lives on land, but they still need water for hydration and reproduction. They don't drink water, they absorb it though their skin, and a ground-level birdbath is a good place to let toads do their absorbing. A child, or curious adult, can even conduct an interesting field study by weighing a "thirsty" toad before and after placing him in the shallow water of a birdbath, or on wet blotter paper, to see how much water-weight he has absorbed through his skin.

Because they grow from their aquatic to terrestrial stage faster than frogs, toads can make do with temporary pools, like the water standing in ditches or spring puddles in the yard, for their egg and tadpole stages, but in some neighborhoods even they are harder and harder to find. On a walk around our block recently my daughter noted that the ditches where she and a friend once collected tadpoles are now piped and dry as a bone. Too bad.

Toads also need hiding places because their enemies are legion. "Almost every meat-eater of the field and forest has a taste for small, easy-to-catch tadpoles," writes one naturalist, and predators like crows, snakes, hawks, owls, and skunks, not to mention cars and lawn mowers, take the adults. Leaving an unmown edge around the lawn provides toad escape routes, and a damp place under a loose brick, a hole under a board, or a cranny under the house provides a home.

In addition to burrowing, playing dead, inflating themselves, and dressing in camouflage (the handsomest toad looks most like a clod of dirt), toads have other defenses. When roughly handled, a toad exudes a sticky, slightly poisonous liquid from his skin, and a dog trying to feast on toad winds up with an inflamed mouth and throat. As 10-year-old Cy Kassoff knows only too well after helping me pose his pet toad for a photograph, toads also have defenses against young boys. "They pee on you," sighs Cy.

But mostly toads just go about their work of bug zapping without fanfare, frying noises, or electricity. And some of them do it for a really long time. One English pet toad—the doyen of bug zappers—reportedly lived to be 36 years old before being eaten by the owner's pet raven.

I like to think my toad companion could live that long, he growing wartier, me grayer, by the year as we rock and sit, rock and sit. "Grow old along with me," wrote a poet who must have known the joys of toad companionship. "The bugs I leave to thee."

June

Staying in the Clover

If you're trying to rid your lawn of clover, hold that herbicide, because you may want to take a fresh look at this useful plant.

Prejudice against clover relates more to what is fashionable than to what is sensible. Seventy years ago, books like *Lawn Making* (1923) were recommending adding white Dutch clover to grass seed, but a generation later we were treating clover as a weed. Fortunately for those of us who have a soft spot for it, clover is making a comeback. It's being recommended for healthy, low-maintenance lawns that use less water and fertilizer than all-grass lawns and for lawns that are wildlife friendly.

The most often cited reason for not including clover in lawns is that its fragrant flowers attract bees. But not everyone sees this as a liability. Providing nectar for honeybees is an asset if you're into wildlife gardening. An occasional barefooted child might be stung by a bee, but most of the children I see tromping through lawns are wearing tennis shoes with treads like tanks. To my mind, a childhood without clover is more to be regretted than a childhood with an occasional bee sting, but I suppose this is a matter of opinion.

And it's a matter of taste, and cultural conditioning, whether you prefer the lumpy look of a lawn enriched with clover to the crew cut look of all fescue. I will admit that the uniformity of an all-grass lawn suits some situations better than a mixture of grass and clover. Where I'm using a ribbon of grass to cut through borders of flowers, I want the grass to be uniform, a place where the eye can rest, not a place complicated with white clover flowers and shamrock-shaped leaves. On the other hand, a large expanse of lawn enriched with clover has a rollicking look that draws me right into it, and not just to look for four-leaf clovers. Such a lawn punctuated with patches of clover suggests "health" to me in a way that a monoculture of fescue maintained with heavy fertilizer, pesticide, and herbicide applications does not.

Clover is as beneficial to lawns as milk is to children. It adds nitrogen to the soil, survives drought and wetness, chokes out weeds, spreads into bare areas, and tolerates heat and cold. UCLA horticulturist Richard Orlando recommends that a "sensibly planned lawn" consist of one quarter to one third clover distributed fairly evenly throughout the turf. Because of its ability to take nitrogen from the air and "fix" it in the soil, clover makes nitrogen available to plants that share the soil with it. Hanover County's Extension Agent Tim Etheredge says that with enough clover in a lawn, you can reduce or possibly even eliminate the need to fertilize with nitrogen.

Clover also benefits animals and butterflies. Wild animals find clover leaves as delectable as do domesticated animals, and clover foliage is an important food for the larval stage of butterflies. To provide good butterfly habitat we need to provide not just nectar sources for the adult butterflies but foods for the butterflies' larval stage as well, and clover is "host plant" to many butterfly species. (Don't worry; butterfly caterpillars seldom cause significant damage to garden plants because they usually feed singly or in small groups.)

Most experts recommend sowing hard, round clover seeds in early spring or fall. Etheredge suggests planting clover in February so it has a chance to freeze, thaw, and work its way into the soil, because it needs good soil contact to germinate. I have planted it in September and had it making a good show by November. The easiest time to introduce it is when your lawn is initially seeded, but you can also overseed existing turf with clover. Overseeding with 1 pound of clover seed per 2,000 square feet is recommended.

The kind to plant is white Dutch clover (*Trifolium repens*), not Ladino clover, which is a giant form of *Trifolium repens* for pastures, or white sweet clover, a biennial with spikes of white flowers that can reach 6 feet.

Clover seeds are available from mail order houses and from most farm feed and seed stores. As often as not, however, in an established lawn, you don't really need to plant clover; it will seed in by itself and all you have to do is avoid wiping it out with broad-leaved weed killers. There may be better ways to make a fortune, but there's no easier way to find yourself "in the clover."

Forget Tree Roses— Grow Roses in Trees

When most people associate roses and trees, they think of tree roses, those highly stylized roses trained to look like balls of bloom on tree-like trunks. But there is another tree-rose association that more people should try: using trees as arbors for roses.

Although nearly everything you read about rose culture will tell you to grow roses in full sun and away from tree roots, a ride down almost any country road will prove that an old climber is willing to clamber up almost anything, including a tree. Red cedars laden with roses are particularly beautiful along Virginia roadsides.

I first began to think seriously about growing climbing roses into trees after reading Vita Sackville-West's garden writing in which she describes using her fruit trees at Sissinghurst as arbors for climbing roses. On a lark, I moved an offshoot of an old climber to a spot under a cherry tree. Imagine my surprise three years later when my cherry tree bloomed—first in white cherry blossoms, then in reddish-pink roses.

Having the cherry tree show off first with its own blooms, then with roses, is a way of deriving maximum "show" from one spot. Long after the birds have picked the tree clean of cherries, the tree is awash in cherry color, because the rose canes, reaching for the sun, have climbed to the top of the tree. My neighbor Nancy Haynes is growing a white climber up a huge old oak tree. She has gotten it to about 15 feet by training it onto twine attached to nails in the tree, and her husband Bruce is already envisioning using the extension ladder to train it higher, because the climber they are growing, *Rosa filipes* 'Kiftsgate,' will climb to 50 feet.

Choosing the site and choosing the right rose are the secrets to growing roses up trees. One sure-fire way to choose the right rose is to get an offshoot of a rose you see growing up a tree in the wild. These old roses usually bloom only once, in the spring, but in my opinion they make up for not blooming longer with their old-fashioned beauty, their fragrance, and their iron constitutions. Look for a rooted offshoot near the base of an old rose, or help the rose root by taking a cane and bending it to the ground, tucking the bend into the soil, and placing a heavy rock or brick on the cane to keep it there. Come back a year later (sometimes sooner) and you will usually find the cane rooted where you tucked it into the soil. Sever it from the parent rose, and voilà—a rose to grow up a tree of your own.

You can also buy some great old ramblers. The one Nancy Haynes is growing, *R. filipes* 'Kiftsgate,' is available from Wayside Gardens. It's an English rose with massive heads of small, sweet-scented, white flowers with bright yellow stamens. It reminds me a little of a refined version of the multiflora rose. The Wayside Gardens catalog describes it as growing up a copper beech at Kiftsgate Court in England where it goes up 40 feet and spreads to 100 feet. 'Paul's Himalayan Musk' is another rambler Wayside Gardens recommends for growing up a tree. It has small pink flowers and will grow to 30 feet. The eglantine rose (*Rosa eglanteria*), which has delicate, pink, single blooms, is another tree-climber.

Once you have found the right rose, you need to site it properly. The goal is to provide it with enough sun, which can be tricky when you're planting under a tree. The branching of a fruit tree is usually open enough to let in enough light to coax a climber to the top of the tree, and once there, the rose can spread out and bloom with abandon. Nancy Haynes has solved the light problem by siting her rose on the open east side of her oak, a tree so tall its canopy creates only high shade anyway.

The most novel solution to the light problem I've ever heard of, however, is one I read about in a *Fine Gardening* article in which gardener David Rigby described first losing three climbers he had tried to coax to the top of an English laurel hedge, because they didn't get enough light. He finally succeeded when he planted the rose at an angle to the ground so that the upper part of the canes received a small amount of light, and then he *ran aluminum foil along the ground,* keeping it there for several months to reflect light up onto the plant. Sounds crazy but it worked. I quote: "The plant now blooms in cascades from 7 ft. to 14 ft. high and calls for mid-season pruning to control it."

What I hope all this suggests to you is possibilities you had never thought of for roses. I know I saw new possibilities this weekend when I visited my daughter, who proudly showed me a rose she was growing almost under a deck where it received little or no direct sunlight. At one time, I would have considered its chances of success nil, but, as Kate pointed out to me, it was throwing one cane skyward, and if that cane ever reaches the deck railing, it will get enough sun and have a chance to grow laterally, which means it will be full of blooms. Throw it a little aluminum foil from the barbecue, and who knows how successful it may be?

Hollyhocks Line the Road to Heaven

The road to heaven isn't paved with gold; it's lined with hollyhocks.
—HELEN MCCONNELL, ASHLAND GARDENER
1901–1989

It is easy to imagine hollyhocks lining the road to heaven because on earth they are so often found growing along narrow passages like alleys and lining paved areas like parking lots. Their tall, upright habit makes them fit such spots as no other plant would, and their proclivity for self-sowing keeps them growing in these neglected places long after the hand that planted them has passed away.

Backyard gardens and farms are equally hospitable to hollyhocks because these old-fashioned flowers are easy to grow. Although plants are available from mail-order houses and nurseries, they are so easy to start from seed, it seems silly to buy plants. You are going to want to grow them from seed eventually anyway because most hollyhocks are biennial and to keep them going you will need to resow them or make sure they reseed themselves. Grow the single-flowered ones, not the doubles. The doubles look too fussy and detract from a plant that doesn't need flowers with extra petals to attract attention. (A double-flowered hollyhock is like a 7-foot man who's changed his hairstyle to attract attention.)

Seeds of old-fashioned, single-flowered hollyhocks used to be hard to find in commerce, but now they are all the rage again and most seed companies sell them. You don't have to buy them, however. Any gardener with hollyhocks is happy to share seeds. The seeds of my favorite hollyhocks, bright, rose-pink beauties, were given me by the proprietor of an antique shop in Harrisonburg who would probably have preferred selling me a rare antique but was more than willing to share seeds of the antique hollyhock blooming near the front door.

The seeds are "packaged" by Mother Nature in a way that makes them particularly easy to carry. About ⅓ inch in diameter, they are lined up like pennies in a roll, but instead of being straight, the roll of hollyhock seeds is connected end to end into a circle, like a doughnut the size of a quarter. Over this roll of seeds is a leafy covering that makes the seeds easy to transport in one's pocket. I have read that the seeds are edible, but I'm not sure at what stage in their development.

Collect the seeds in late July or in August when they're fully ripe; their leafy covering will be gray and dry. They can be planted immediately, in the fall, or in early spring. In a mild winter, the foliage of plants that germinated in late summer or early fall will be almost evergreen, but harsher winters will kill their foliage almost to the ground. The plants will fill out the following spring and bloom first in late May or June, then sporadically throughout the summer. Always be sure to have some new plants coming along because the old ones will die. As often as not, however, in a congenial spot, hollyhocks will drop seeds all around them, and new plants will emerge almost at the base of the old ones.

They grow best in full sun and are less likely to require staking where they get bright light on all sides. Growing to 6 feet, they make a great backdrop for almost any border, but I particularly like them growing along fences. In downtown Richmond, there used to be a row of hollyhocks growing along a fence made of old doors stacked lengthwise, a wonderful sight. If you condition them properly, you can also use hollyhocks as cut flowers. A 6-foot hollyhock stalk doesn't want to hold its tip up after it's been cut, but if you will cut it in the morning, prop it against something that helps its tip stay erect, and let it soak up water overnight, it will droop, then reconstitute itself before morning.

Crimson, rose-pink, light pink, and ivory are the most common hollyhock flower colors, but they also come in primrose yellow and even black. The black ones sound awful, but I begged one from a neighbor to have on hand for an arranging workshop recently, and someone combined it with the feathery flowers of white goatsbeard in an arrangement that was as dramatic as it was beautiful. Funnel-shaped hollyhock flowers can also be made into hollyhock ladies. Here's how: leaving a bit of stem on it, pick a hollyhock blossom and position it with the edge of the petals down. This will be the lady's skirt and body. Then pick an unopened bud and carefully remove its green covering, including all of the calyx and stem parts. Revealed will be a tight, round, colored ball of petals with four holes at the base. Two of these holes will be your hollyhock lady's eyes. Into the largest of the remaining holes, slide the stem of the flower that is your lady's skirt. If you wish, place a Canterbury bell or bellflower bonnet on your hollyhock lady's head and send her off to church to hear Jack-in-the-Pulpit. This will prepare her for her later role as sentinel along the road to heaven.

Rethinking Rhododendrons

"I have grown tired of the harvest I myself desired," Robert Frost wrote in a poem about apple-picking—and human ambition—but I think of it every time I look at my rhododendrons. When I bought them in half-gallon pots, I never thought I would live long enough to see them grow to the size of those I loved in the woodland behind my childhood home. But not only have I lived long enough to see them reach their mature size, I have lived long enough to grow tired of the blossoms I myself desired.

Don't get me wrong; these large shrubs with handsome, evergreen foliage and enormous globes of flowers can be strikingly beautiful in the right setting. The right setting is a place where their flowers won't be out of proportion to what is around them. They're beautiful in a woodland setting under tall trees where the added green of what is around them keeps the proportion of leaf to flower from being too skewed in favor of flower. They also bloom at a nice time, after most of the azaleas have faded. But if these same shrubs happen to be backing a small garden of delicate wildflowers, for example, you'll wish their blooms away because they're just too big and gawky, especially the magenta-flowered ones, not to outshine their neighbors. "If I'd had time, I'd have gone and ripped the blooms off mine before you came," Nancy Arrington told me only half in jest last week as I toured her native plant garden, because she shares my prejudice against these flowers.

But if you've just planted rhododendrons or are about to, this isn't what you want to hear. You want to know how to plant them, keep them healthy, and grow them to blooming size as quickly as possible. Here's how.

First of all, make sure you're buying a rhododendron hardy for your area. Among the hardiest rhododendrons, those called "ironclads," are those with "roseum" and "catawbiense" in their names. The magenta flowered 'English Roseum,' for example, is as tough as nails. So is *Rhododendron catawbiense* 'Album,' which has white flowers flushed with lilac. A hardy rhododendron with fragrant pink flowers is 'Cadis,' and 'Annuh Kruske' is a hardy one with lavender flowers.

Next, choose a well-drained site because poor drainage is the thing most likely to kill a rhododendron or to weaken it so that something else can kill it. The list of diseases and pests that bother rhododendron is as long as my arm, but you can avoid most of them with good cultural practices.

In addition to a well-drained site, choose one with acidic soil, some shelter from winter wind, and partial shade. Rhododendrons are understory shrubs, growing in bright shade under tall trees in their native habitats, so try to plant them where conditions are similar. ('Cadis,' 'P.J.M.,' and 'Cynthia' are among the cultivars that can take more sun than most rhododendrons.) Rhododendrons also prefer soil enriched with organic matter, so try to give them the same humus-rich conditions they would enjoy in an ancient forest.

Plant them shallow, with their root balls even with the surface of the surrounding soil or perhaps slightly higher. So important is shallow planting to rhododendrons that Chesterfield nurseryman Bert Shoosmith, who propagated his first rhododendron in 1940, once conducted an experiment to prove it. He planted 12 rhododendrons traditionally, with their root balls in the ground, then he "planted" 12 more by placing their root balls on top of the ground, surrounding them with nothing more than mulch. Three years later, he had lost none of the rhododendrons set on top of the ground but had lost two of those planted in holes.

Shoosmith says they need little fertilizer; I would agree, having never fertilized the ones that now tower over my head. He recommends "a light touch" of organic fertilizer in early spring, a light mulch with an acidic material like pine needles, and water during summer dry spells. To save the plant's energy, he also recommends deadheading, cutting off the old blossoms after they have bloomed.

How to Grow Grandmother's Roses—Without a Grandmother

This is a discussion of old roses, but it will have nothing to say about albas, damasks, or gallicas. Those are some of the names that help rosarians understand the lineage of old roses, but I'm more interested in roses with pedigrees like this: "it came from my grandmother's house."

These are the roses that explode with bloom in May or June then do little if any blooming the rest of the year. They are the roses with no names that bloom in inner city backyards and on country fences. They are the roses that seem to flourish with no attention and keep blooming long after anyone has thought about fertilizing them. They are the roses that always belong to somebody else.

"I don't know where it came from," says Betty Tharrington of the climbing rose laden with pink blooms on her arbor. "It was here when we bought the house. It just blooms one time a year. I whack it back in the fall so the wind doesn't whip it, and I cut out the dead wood in the fall. It likes where it is."

"It doesn't have a name," says Mrs. Joan Priddy of the old pink rose on her back fence. "Years and years ago we decided everybody in the Ashland Garden Club would get the same rose. I think it had a number; it didn't have a name. It's been here 45 years. I haven't done one thing to it except put cow manure on it. My things don't get much attention."

"It came from my grandmother's house," says Randy Doggett of the rose bush covered with pink blooms in his front yard. Randy even has a note to prove it. Entitled "History of Rose Bush," the note from his mother says the rose in his front yard, planted in 1966, is an offspring of a bush that grew along his grandmother's fence in Doswell. That rose, purchased from Miller and Rhoads Department Store in 1947, still thrives in Doswell.

Old roses. If you didn't inherit one with your house or from your grandmother, how do you get one? There are nurseries that specialize in old roses and most of the catalogs that carry perennials and ornamental shrubs have also begun to carry old roses, but if you want a rose exactly like the one in the Doggett's front yard, Mrs. Priddy's back yard, or Betty Tharrington's side yard, the only way to get it, short of theft, is to propagate it yourself.

Here's how to do it. First, look to see if the rose has sent out underground stems from which an offshoot plant is growing. If it has, you can sever this offspring from the parent plant. Many ramblers also take root where their canes touch the ground and you can sever these rooted offspring from the parent plant. If an old rose with flexible canes hasn't produced offspring this way itself, you can induce it to do so by the process called soil layering.

The simplest version of soil layering is placing a rock or brick over a flexible cane tucked into the earth as described in "Forget Tree Roses—Grow Roses in Trees." With many roses, that's all you need to do to get a rooted offshoot. But you can speed up the process and ensure a greater success rate by wounding the cambium before burying the cane. In spring or early summer, bend a long cane over and note where it would touch the ground about a foot from its tip. Excavate that spot to a depth of about 6 inches and fill it with a mixture of half coarse sand and half peat. Then, into the lower side of the cane, make a shallow, slicing cut through the bark and cambium about a foot from the cane's tip. Strip the leaves from either side of the cut, moisten the cut and dust it with a rooting hormone (some growers leave out this step), and prop something like a tooth-pick in the cut to keep it partially open. Then, bend the cane over until the wounded part of the cane reaches the spot filled with the sand-peat mixture. Make a furrow, bury the nicked part of the cane in it, and cover with soil. Use a forked stick or weighty object like a brick or rock to hold the cane down. Keep moist. Roots will develop in the area of the cut, and, when they do, you can sever the new plant from the parent plant.

Another way to reproduce a rose exactly is to take softwood cuttings in June or July. As soon as the roses' petals start to fall off, cut off the upper few inches of a flowering stem just above a 5-leaflet leaf. Then make another diagonal cut about 5 inches farther down the stem. Remove all the leaves except the upper pair. Plant the cutting in a pot filled with a mixture of half coarse sand and half peat. (Some gardeners dust the ends of their cuttings with a rooting hormone before sticking them in the sand-peat mix; others report equal or greater success without it.) Water well and cover the pot and cutting with a plastic bag sealed by tucking it under the pot (or put pot and cutting in a zip-lock bag). Put your covered cutting in a bright spot but out of direct sunlight. The inside of the bag will steam up like a shower curtain, but that's what you want: a nice humid little greenhouse. Watch the cutting until new shoots appear, in four to eight weeks, then remove the plastic bag gradually by opening it for longer and longer periods each day. Repot the rooted cutting in a good soil mixture and keep it in a cool, shaded spot for about three weeks. Gradually move it out into the kind of light and temperature conditions it will experience in the garden before planting it there.

At this point, don't assume you have succeeded. It takes a lot of attention and patience to grow a tiny rooted cutting into an heirloom rose, and the last time I congratulated myself on planting out rooted rose cuttings, they were mowed down by an overzealous teenage groundskeeper within a week. Guard them well.

I have cuttings from the Doggett's rose bush rooting in their plastic bag greenhouses on my back porch right now, and I have faith they'll grow into my children's heirloom roses. Does it matter that I'll have to tell my children they came from the Doggett's grandmother and not their own? Not a bit. When it comes to roses, a grandmother is a grandmother is a grandmother.

Plant Labels: Make Mine Invisible

In botanical gardens, where they serve a teaching function, plant labels should be conspicuous, but most everywhere else, I want them to be invisible. Nothing spoils a planting you want to look natural—as if Mother Nature had planted it herself—faster than a white plastic label.

June

Plant labels and markers serve two functions: they remind you what you have planted and where. Almost every gardener has used "low-tech" location markers of one sort or another— a stockade of sticks around a seedling, a gray rock set against red earth above a bulb. I noticed a fine collection of pencils in front of my daughter's fence last weekend marking spots where she had planted baby glads and didn't want the condo grounds-keeper to mow them down.

But we usually want location markers to be visible to us, the gardeners, and invisible to everyone else. Golf tees make great markers of the invisible kind. I learned about using golf tees from Brent Heath of the Daffodil Mart, who suggests using them to mark the locations of bulbs whose foliage disappears. Although they come in colors that are anything but inconspicuous (golfers didn't have camouflage in mind when they invented them), they slip easily into the soil, and if you push them deep enough, they're invisible to anyone who isn't looking for them.

But what about labels you need to remind you of plant names? Most plant names should go in a garden journal, not in the garden. A notation like "planted meadow rue to the left of white violets on north side of house near downspout" works as well as, and looks better than, a label. If journaling isn't for you, make your label as inconspicuous as possible. That is unless, like famed British gardener Gertrude Jekyll, you want to make your plant labels as big and ugly as possible as a self-inflicted penance to continue until you learn their names!

Some zinc and galvanized steel markers, on which you can imprint the name of your plant with a nail or ballpoint pen, can be pushed almost completely into the earth and pulled up only when you need a reminder. Popsicle sticks sharpened to a point and other wooden markers have the advantage of at least being made out of natural material, but untreated wood takes up moisture and your writing on it may become illegible in a matter of months. Hanover gardener Jerry Huntsinger, for example, was once given a truckload of cacti by an Arizona horticulturist who, as payment, asked only that Jerry report back on how well the cacti did in Virginia. A year later when Jerry went to fulfill his end of the bargain, all the names he'd written on his wooden markers with permanent black ink were gone.

For indelible labels, some gardeners use labeling wheels that emboss letters on plastic tape. Then they staple the tape to wooden stakes. "You can read the bumps even after the ink's washed off," says Gwen Huntsinger.

White plastic labels are easy to write on with pencil, and the names can be scrubbed off for the markers' reuse, but plastic markers get brittle with age, can't take impacts, and look like trash in the garden. The only places I like to see them are in flats of seedlings and in vegetable gardens where "the hand of man" is obvious anyway and labels seem crucial to the process. Vegetable gardeners are often growing more than one variety of the same plant, for example, and the labels serve the same teaching-comparison function they do in botanical gardens.

I also like to see decorative porcelain markers in herb gardens, because there, too, markers seem appropriate, perhaps because the herbs have traditionally been used medicinally and one wouldn't want Brother Cadfael to mix them up. Porcelain markers are really fragile, however, and I still rue the day my misplaced foot broke a special one my son had given me. Where will I ever again find a porcelain plant label proclaiming "Weeds"?

July

No-Sweat Choice: Purple Coneflowers

What most gardeners want in July are flowers that need no attention. They want flowers they can smile at on the way to the air-conditioned car. They want plants that are drought tolerant, since rain is a sometime thing in July, and they want plants with flowers they can cut and bring inside where it's cool.

If just such a low-maintenance, July-loving plant is what you're looking for, I have the plant for you. It's the purple coneflower, an adaptable wildflower that is as attractive as it is stalwart. It's native to open woods and prairies in much of the south and central United States, but the first one I ever saw was blooming in a formal garden, where I thought it was the most elegant flower I had ever seen. Its mauve-pink petals swept gracefully back from the central disk, and the flower stood as straight on its tall, stiff stem as a patrician with his nose in the air. Imagine my surprise, then, when I later heard a horticulturist describe the purple coneflower as "dingy, coarse, and wholly out of place in self-respecting gardens." Was the man mad?

Possibly, or maybe he was just looking at an old purple coneflower, because purple coneflowers do have a tendency to outlive their beauty. The flowers refuse to die and unless you cut them off, they will stick around looking dull, ragged, and worn out for weeks past their prime. It's easy enough to cut the spent blooms off—just dash out of the air-conditioned house *for a minute*—and fresh new blooms will follow them. Some flower arrangers even make the best of worn out purple coneflowers by removing petals that have been nibbled or torn and using the plant's attractive cones alone in arrangements. Like the fresh flowers, these cones are particularly valuable to arrangers, because they stand on tall, 2- to 4-foot, stiff stems.

Echinacea, the purple coneflower's genus name, comes from the Greek word "echinos" for hedgehog and alludes to the cone's texture. Its spines, actually disk flowers, are so stiff the cones were once used as hair combs, and combflower is another of the plant's common names. Up close, at one stage in their development, these spines are slightly orange with red tips, and they add a really interesting color contrast to the flower's mauve-pink petals.

Purple coneflowers (*Echinacea purpurea*) are only one of several *Echinacea* species native to the United States, and many of them have been used medicinally for centuries. Botanist Steven Foster, who has made a life's work of studying them, says plants of the genus *Echinacea* have been used to treat more ailments than any other plant. Plains Indians reportedly kept *Echinacea* root as handy as we do aspirin, and even today Richmond health food store owners say this is one their most popular herbal remedies. The label on bottles of Echinacea capsules (which contain the root powder) describe it as promoting well-being during the cold and flu season. *Echinacea* root has a numbing effect when chewed. Try it; it's not as numbing as Novocain but does slightly deaden the mouth, and it has been used to treat everything from colds to cancer. In fact, so popular have *Echinacea* root remedies become that in 1994 Missouri had to pass a law to keep poachers from collecting *Echinacea* roots on public land.

Root poachers are no problem in my garden, but I do collect the flowers by the score. From mid-June until October, purple coneflowers bloom. A single plant can provide as many as twenty flowers at a time, a single flower, albeit tattered, can last as long as a month. And the flowers are remarkably easy to grow. Purple coneflowers like full sun or part shade and can even compete with weeds in a meadow situation. The plants are finicky only about having well-drained soil—the plant's roots will rot in soil that stays wet—and although they reputedly prefer neutral to alkaline soils, my purple coneflowers thrive in slightly acid soil. Plants are available from most wildflower and perennial nurseries, but they are also easy to grow from seed as long as you realize the seeds need a cold period to break their dormancy. Plant them in the fall, let winter provide the cold period, and they will germinate the following spring.

Once you have purple coneflowers established in the yard, the plant will also self-sow, and you'll have enough seedlings to move wherever you want them. Remember where you plant them, however, because the plant is a bit slow to send up leaves in the spring, and it's easy to plant something else on top. Be aware, too, that you may get some strange flowers from self-sown purple coneflowers—flowers with stubby, green petals or with cones that have strange "witches broom" appendages jutting out from them. I have a neighbor who loves to use these oddities in arrangements, but were it not for her liking them, I would pull these mutant coneflowers out.

Butterflies, on the other hand, are a coneflower bonus everybody appreciates. They bask on the cones and sip from the nectar-rich flowers. So common is it to see a butterfly on a purple coneflower that the butterfly's upswept wings begin to seem as organic to the flower's form as its own back-swept petals. Birds like purple coneflowers, too; they eat the seeds that form after the flowers, so you will want to leave some of these ripe cones standing into the fall and winter. Think of them not as spent flowers but as bird feeders that fill themselves.

Flierworks! Watch Butterflies on the Fourth

It may not be as well known as the Audubon Society's Christmas bird count, but the Xerces Society's Fourth of July butterfly count is a great opportunity for amateur naturalists to hone their butterfly watching skills. The purpose of the count is to raise butterfly awareness and enjoyment, and, of course, to document the number of butterflies of particular species in a given area. But even backyard butterfly watchers who don't know a swallowtail from a skipper can add something to the state of butterfly knowledge by watching the behavior of butterflies in their yards.

That there is more to butterfly behavior than we usually notice was brought home to me by Robert Michael Pyle's wonderful *Handbook for Butterfly Watchers* (1992). Without a single color illustration, Pyle proves, "even were they gray creatures, nameless and scattered randomly over the landscape, butterflies would still be wholly worth attending to for their behavior alone."

Butterfly flight patterns vary, for example. They fly at

different speeds and have different ways of stroking their wings. There is the "powerful sailing of the swallowtails," the "maddening darting of the hairstreaks," the "flapping of the sulphurs." Butterflies even differ in their reaction to being disturbed. According to Pyle, a disturbed angelwing, skipper, or hairstreak will tend to return to its perch, but if sulphurs and swallowtails have been frightened away, they are most likely lost from sight.

Pyle discusses where and how to look for butterflies. A meadow, or even an infrequently mowed easement, where butterflies can bask in the sun and absorb the warmth they need for flight, is one of the best places. Mud puddles attract male butterflies who gather there in what are called "drinking clubs." Scientists, unsure why these drinking clubs form, think the butterflies may be after mineral salts in the water. Rotten fruit and animal scat—the fresher the better—attract butterflies, as does urine, a phenomenon Pyle says a butterfly watcher can use to his advantage, social conditions permitting.

And, of course, we can watch butterflies in our own gardens, particularly if we have planted the nectar sources that attract them. Flower nectar is the main food of adult butterflies, but certain flowers are more attractive to butterflies than others. The best butterfly flowers not only provide ample nectar but also are shaped in a way that allows the butterfly's proboscis easy access to the nectar and gives the butterfly a place to perch comfortably as it sips. Among the best garden flowers to grow for butterflies are aster, zinnia, verbena, liatris, lantana, purple coneflower, butterfly weed, coreopsis, and black-eyed Susan, but the quintessential butterfly plant is butterfly bush.

The most widely grown butterfly bush is *Buddleia davidii*, a shrub with long arching branches, silvery gray foliage, and tightly packed clusters of tubular flowers that look something like lilac blossoms, hence the plant's other common name "summer lilac." The flowers of the original butterfly bush species are bluish purple with orange centers, but horticultural varieties come in colors from violet to deep purple, white, and pink. They all like full sun and will grow in almost any well-drained soil. Fritillaries, swallowtails, red admirals, and painted ladies are particularly fond of butterfly bush, but the list of butterflies visiting this shrub could be longer. One English naturalist reported counting as many as a dozen species of butterflies visiting her butterfly bush on a single July day!

Binoculars or a net for capturing butterflies will help you examine them up close. Many natural history museums carry inexpensive (about $4) butterfly nets or you can make your own with a pole, wire coat hanger, and cheesecloth. According to Pyle, chasing butterflies with a net seldom works; they are "much more fleet and graceful than we." Instead, he says, wait patiently for the butterfly to perch on the ground, then clamp the net quickly over it, or wait until it lights on a flower, then swoop it up into the net.

Although some rare butterflies should never be collected, even conservationists like Pyle condone capturing common butterflies for collections. Pyle says collecting should be done with respect, and that specimens should be dignified with accurate labels, but he sees collecting common, backyard species as doing more good than harm if it raises butterfly awareness. Another reason collecting common species isn't frowned upon is that butterflies reproduce their numbers so rapidly that taking individual butterflies doesn't have much impact on a healthy population. "Predators—from spiders to dragonflies to birds—have infinitely greater speed, appetite, and success than all the collectors put together. And automobiles, lawn mowers, and garden sprays kill more than collectors do," writes Pyle.

Not only that, but in the wild, butterflies live a surprisingly short time. According to Pyle, although some robust swallowtails live a month or two, the average adult butterfly lives only about two weeks, and some dainty species live only a few days.

If you have no appetite for collecting but want to get up close and personal with butterflies (their iridescent scales are spectacular viewed with a hand lens), try looking on the grills of cars for butterfly wings. I spent many an hour conducting such searches as I did high school parking lot duty and have an impressive collection of butterfly wings to show for it. (My principal thought I was looking for drugs.)

In the field, there's also as much joy to be had from leaving a butterfly undisturbed as from collecting it. Writes Pyle, "I feel a special satisfaction in leaving a butterfly undisturbed after watching it well."

Although a butterfly field guide would be more useful in teaching a beginner to identify butterfly species, Pyle's *Handbook for Butterfly Watchers* provides a general description of the major butterfly groups and notes that an amateur should be able to identify about three-quarters of the almost 700 species in North America. Backyard butterfly watchers can even add to butterfly knowledge by documenting the species they see. Although everyone seems to think butterfly populations have diminished, and some species have declined to the point of extinction, others have actually benefited from human activities.

So pull up your lawn chair and study those backyard butterflies. Their show is as good as a fireworks display, and you don't have to wait for the sun to go down to see it.

Butterfly Weed or Chigger Weed?

"What's that you're buying?" a friend of Sue Robertson's asked when she saw Sue buying a plant with orange blooms. "A piece of my childhood," Sue answered.

For Ashland gardener Sue Robertson, the plant with flat umbels of orange blooms that most of us call butterfly weed is the plant that she had always wanted to pick as a child but was never allowed to. "It's got chiggers," adults always warned her.

Sue now has several plants of butterfly weed in her garden. One of them is the size of a small azalea and looks like an airport when butterflies are landing on it. As far as I know, Sue has no chiggers, but there may have been a thread of truth in the advice she received as a child.

Chigger weed is one of the common names for *Asclepias tuberosa*, otherwise known as butterfly weed. It is possible the plant acquired that name because its blooms can be red-orange like chiggers. But chiggers, parasitic mites that feed on us and leave a "straw" behind that makes us itch, are so small as to be nearly invisible, so it's unlikely that enough people have seen a chigger's color to be naming a plant for it. It's more likely the adults in Sue Robertson's childhood called this plant chigger weed because the plant often grows where chiggers lurk. Chiggers lurk on grass stems, leaves, and shrubbery, usually in dry sunny spots on woods' edges—exactly where you'd expect to find butterfly weed. Chiggers also tend to congregate in what are called "mite islands"; that is, one spot in an area may be full of chiggers when a nearby spot of apparently equal attraction to them can be chigger free. I'm told one of the best defenses against chiggers is to keep moving. "You'll get a few chiggers while moving, but sitting on the ground in chigger territory is really asking for it," says naturalist E. F. Rivinus, so stopping to pick chigger weed in chigger territory might not have been such a good idea.

Fortunately for those who enjoy butterfly weed as ornamentals and as cut flowers, these native wildflowers are as happy in perennial borders as they are in chigger territory. Although bright orange butterfly weed is the norm, plants are available in a range of colors from red to orange and yellow. Blooming in June and July, or later, especially if the plants have been mowed or cut, butterfly weed's flat clusters (umbels) of flowers appear at the top of 1- to 3-foot stems. Each floret is shaped like a milkweed flower—cinched in the middle like a belted torso. (Although it lacks the milky exudation of most milkweeds, butterfly weed is, in fact, a milkweed.) Not only is each one of these florets filled with nectar relished by butterflies, but the florets' arrangement provides butterflies a perfect landing pad and a place to bask as they soak up the solar heat they need to raise their body temperatures and give them power for flight.

Growing butterfly weed is easy, but it requires some patience. Whatever you do, don't try to dig butterfly weed from the wild. Not only is it a conservation "no-no," it's unlikely to work. Butterfly weed (*Asclepias tuberosa*) has a long, brittle tap root that is easily damaged and does not like to be moved. The best way to get butterfly weed started in the garden is to grow it from seed or to buy small, container-grown plants. You can purchase seeds from seed catalogs or collect them from the wild, with permission of the landowner. Like other members of the milkweed family, butterfly weed has long (4- to 5-inch) seed pods that split open to release flat, dark brown seeds with a fluff of down on the end. The fluff helps wind disperse the seeds, sometimes lifting them into the air before you have had time to collect them. Wildflower expert Harry Phillips suggests that if you can't check the pods frequently enough to see if they are mature and are afraid they will split open and spill their seeds in your absence, you can tie a string around the center of the pod to prevent it from losing its seeds as it splits.

I find butterfly weed remarkably easy to start from seed; the seeds don't require a cold period to germinate and almost all of them come up. What is hard about growing butterfly weed from seed is not germinating the seed but having the patience and vigilance to grow the seedling to flowering size. I try to get butterfly weed seedlings in the ground while the plants are small, before their roots will feel the transplant shock. Or, I plant seeds directly where they are to grow, but it can take two years for butterfly weed to reach flowering size, so it's easy to forget where a butterfly weed seedling is and "do it in" with an errant hoe. Butterfly weed is also one of those plants that disappears completely during its dormant season and is late to emerge in spring, so mark the location of your plants carefully. Because the plants don't like to be moved, you will also want to locate them with appropriate companions from the start. My favorite companion for butterfly weed is lavender-blue Stokes' aster (*Stokesia laevis*), which blooms at the same time and also attracts butterflies. Coreopsis (*Coreopsis* spp.) makes another good butterfly weed companion.

Butterfly weed likes plenty of sun and well-drained soil. Once established, the plants are long-lived and drought tolerant. Harry Phillips recommends butterfly weed for roadside planting because it recovers quickly from mowing; mowed in May, it will bloom by July, and he says nothing is quite as striking as "a few clumps of butterfly weed spotted in an expanse of green lawn."

Because butterfly weed makes a great cut flower but shouldn't be picked in the wild, it is also a good plant to add to the cutting garden where it will supply "legal" cut flowers. Both its color and form are dramatic in arrangements, and I've used it in everything from mass arrangements to bridesmaids' bouquets. One caveat: if anyone about to march down an aisle carrying it should ask you what it is, it's wiser to call it butterfly weed than chigger weed.

Beset by Bees? Run Away!

The first time a bumblebee stung me while I was gardening I was shocked and indignant. Where had he come from and what had I done wrong? But there was no time to linger in confusion, because he was trying to sting me again. I tried to knock him away; no luck. I tried to bob and weave to avoid him; no luck. I tried to run away, but he stayed right with me. My husband finally rescued me by chasing us both down and swatting the bee away with his hat.

Bees can sting only once, you say? Not bumblebees. Unlike most other bees, bumblebees can and will sting more than once. I shouldn't have needed an expert to confirm what experience had already taught me, but my knowledge was reinforced by these words I found in a field guide shortly after my bumblebee encounter: "Bumblebees are not disemboweled by stinging and are therefore able to sting repeatedly. And because they are generally large and sturdy, they are less likely to be injured in the fray than their more delicate cousins."

Another expert, my neighbor who has experienced mad dogs, rabid raccoons, and rattlesnakes but saves his most terrifying tones for stories about bees, had this to say about bumblebees: "Yeah, you tangle with one of them black ones and it'll run you for a mile."

The more time anyone spends outdoors, the more healthy a respect he or she gains for bees, but bumblebees had always been the bees I was least afraid of. They seemed so slow, so fat and furry, so friendly, as bees go. One article I'd read in a gardening magazine described them as "quite shy"; another, entitled "The Beloved Bumbler," began "Can any gardener help but like bumblebees?"

No, you can't help liking them—until they sting you. I have spent hours picking larkspur from under bumblebees' noses and have stared down many a bumblebee daring me to weed around my hollyhocks. I intend to continue doing those things, but now that I have experienced the bumblebee's dark side, I don't have the "don't-bother-them-and-they-won't-bother-you" attitude I once had. Sometimes bees come out of nowhere and hit you hard; that's a fact. So when I felt a bee fly up my pant leg recently, it was not with a gentle whack but with a ferocious blow that I smacked him dead under the cloth. Another bumblebee, as it turned out.

I have also read that our natural tendency to run away from attacking bees is the correct response. The bees are chasing intruders away from a hive or nest, so we can reduce our chances of being stung by heeding their "request" to move along. Not only that, but according to biologist Adrian Forsyth, the poison glands of bees, and possibly wasps, release a pheromone, an airborne scent that attracts other bees and incites them to sting, so if you're stung and remain near the hive or nest, it is likely you will be stung again.

If you spend much time in bee territory, and most gardeners do, you might want to have on hand a nifty little device called a venom extractor. It's a plastic device that looks like a hypodermic needle except that it has a suction cup instead of a needle on the end. You put it over the sting, and when you depress the plunger, a vacuum is created over the wound. Almost painlessly, it draws up the skin, venom, and sometimes a little blood. I'd had little faith in this device until I used one and felt it almost miraculously ease the pain of a sting. Look for venom extractors in stores that sell outdoor equipment and in catalogs that sell camping gear. If you expect to tangle with bumblebees, you want one.

Stiff No More: Clip the Funeral Look Out of Glads

When writer Phyllis Theroux moved to Ashland, she wasted no time giving new form to an old cliché. She took her scissors to the familiar "I love Ashland" bumper sticker and rearranged the words to read "Ashland I love."

Such a makeover is just what I recommend for gladioli.* So accustomed are we to seeing glads used in what I call the Statue of Liberty arrangement—fanned out like the points in Lady Liberty's crown—that funeral baskets of glads arranged in this way have become almost a cliché. But it is as easy to clip the cliché from glads as it is to do it with a bumper sticker.

---

*The only things stiffer than a gladiolus in a funeral arrangement are the proper plural forms of the word: *gladioli* and *gladioluses*. While some dictionaries accept the singular form *gladiola* as an alternative to *gladiolus*, they do not accept the plural form *gladiolas*. Too bad, because gardeners are much more comfortable growing gladiolas—or glads—than they are growing either gladioli or gladioluses.

Ashland arranger Brenda Gilman taught me how to "deconstruct" a gladiolus. With a snip of the clippers one can turn a sword of gladiolus flowers and buds into two, three, or even more "florets." A cut just above the lowest flower, for example, results in a single flower on a long stem. And because it's not on a spike of flowers just like it, it looks decidedly un-gladioluslike. Such a flower can be used not just in mass arrangements but as one might use a single iris in an oriental or other sparse arrangement. Another snip somewhere up the stem results in shorter-stemmed flowers that can be used as one uses camellias, and the remaining shortened wand of flowers and buds can be used as a miniature glad.

Even without deconstructing a gladiolus one can make these flowers look less stiff and predictably swordlike by keeping them from being the tallest flowers in arrangements. For example, if you can find taller flowers like Queen Anne's lace or dill weed to rise above your glads, you'll avoid the Statue of Liberty look and give your glads a fresh face. Ornamental grasses soften the stiff look of glads, too, particularly when they rise above the swords.

Glads are both easy to find sold as cut flowers and easy to grow yourself. One reason they're so easy to grow is that the corms we receive in the mail or purchase at the hardware store were presumably grown by experts, giving us a healthy product to begin with. (Most bulbs come to us with this stored potential for success.) If you plant new corms every year in a sunny spot with well-drained, moderately rich soil, glads are almost no-fail. The only challenge is keeping them upright, because they want to topple. Although I think a carefully staked glad is a thing of beauty, I have no patience for it and take toppling as a sign a glad is ready to be cut.

And I grow glads for cutting. Although I have heard they can be used to fill bare spots in the perennial border and to fill holes left by bulbs like tulips and daffodils, I have yet to see them effectively used that way. To my mind they belong in the vegetable garden, like other crops one is planning to harvest.

July

With a winter mulch, some glads are hardy in zones 7 to 9, but to be safe, many gardeners in zone 7 dig glads after their foliage has yellowed, about six weeks after flowering, and store the corms dry over the winter in a 40 to 50°F place. Replanting them in a new spot every year also gives the corms the "fresh soil" they like. My neighbor Nancy Sherrod, however, has stunning 5-foot glads that stay in the ground all winter and come back reliably every year. She attributes their endurance to having planted the corms 8 to 10 inches deep as opposed to the 5 inches recommended. A botanist friend tells me, however, that glads adjust to their preferred soil depth by pulling themselves down if planted shallow, or by forming new corms atop old ones if planted deep, so I'm not sure Nancy's theory is correct.

What cannot be disputed is the performance of her glads. Although Nancy's glads bloom all at once, a situation that can be avoided if you plant them at two week intervals, what a show they make while they're blooming! Purple, red, bright pink, yellow, cream, and salmon—they're a spectacle even a gardener with sedate boxwood tastes couldn't resist. If you think you're too sophisticated to be swayed by such a spectacle, think again. I once thought these flowers too showy for my taste, but now that I know how to clip the cliché out of them, gladioli I love.

Rose of Sharon Is Indomitable

Maybe I associate Rose of Sharon with hard times because of *The Grapes of Wrath*. In Steinbeck's novel about migrant workers, the Joad family's daughter is named Rose of Sharon, "Rosasharn" to her mother, whose "mouth loved the name of her daughter." Whether Ma Joad took the name from the Bible (Song of Solomon 2:1) or from the shrub, I don't know, but it is an appropriate name in a family as indomitable as the shrub.

Rose of Sharon (*Hibiscus syriacus*) will endure poor soil, hot weather, and neglect. Truth be told, most horticulturists don't

103

like it; they find it weedy and berate it for producing too many seedlings, for lacking fall color, and for leafing out too late in the spring. But this is like despising the Joads for being poor. More essential to the Joads' and to this shrub's character is that they endure hard times and "bloom" under the worst of conditions.

Rose of Sharon looks its best only in the hottest part of summer. Blooming from July to September, it looks perky and robust when the rest of the garden looks wilted and worn out. Often its performance is all the more surprising because the gardener may not have even known he had a Rose of Sharon until it bloomed! I don't know why—because these shrubs grow so fast, because they look so inconspicuous before they bloom, or because they seed in so surreptitiously?—but Rose of Sharon seems to spring full-blown from the earth.

The shrub's flowers resemble a hollyhock's, and I presume the plant is sometimes called "shrub Althea" because *Althaea* is the former genus name for hollyhocks. Rose of Sharon's flowers are funnel-shaped with five white, red, pink, or bluish-purple petals, often with a darker-colored "eye" at the center. They can be single, semi-double, or double, and some of the doubles look almost like camellia blossoms. Because it grows so fast, Rose of Sharon is inexpensive (it's often the freebie that mail-order houses send out with other orders), and when young, it's easy to transplant. It likes a sunny spot with moist, well-drained soil enriched with peat moss, leaf mold, or compost, but it tolerates partial shade and will grow in almost any soil that is not too dry or too wet.

Gardeners often grow Rose of Sharon standing alone, like a specimen plant, but if you have no room for a one-season specimen shrub, you can sneak Rose of Sharon into a hedge of other shrubs, where it will take up virtually no space, visual or physical, until it blooms. If you are worried about its seeding into other parts of the garden, plant one of the modern, sterile hybrids.

At first Rose of Sharon has a stiff, upright habit, but as the shrubs mature, they spread out and get bushier. Although smaller, rangy, shrubs are more typical, a mature Rose of Sharon can reach 12 feet tall with a 10-foot spread.

A stunning, 8-foot Rose of Sharon with lavender, semi-double flowers blooms in front of an elegant row house near the southeast corner of Richmond's Strawberry Street and Stuart Avenue. In that setting, the shrub looks almost ritzy. But the Rose of Sharon I enjoy most grows beside a tumbledown dwelling on the road to Fork Union. There, against a background of peeling paint, it blooms its heart out—a demonstration of character worthy of Steinbeck.

At War with Japanese Beetles

This is no time of year for a pacifist. This is the time of year when even peace-loving folks are dreaming of death and destruction. The issue in July is not whether to love the enemy or to bury him; it's whether to trap him, poison him, or inflict him with a deadly disease.

How do gardeners get so bellicose? Well, the summer I waged my most destructive battle against Japanese beetles I did it because I realized I had never seen my white crepe myrtles in full bloom. Every summer prior to that one, I had let the Japanese beetles have their way with my crepe myrtles, then enjoyed whatever ragged blooms were left. But the summer I sprayed, Japanese beetles were devouring a particularly promising bunch of buds, and I decided to go after them. I used the napalm of insecticides, Sevin, which is a broad spectrum insecticide that kills beneficial as well as harmful insects. How I convinced myself to do this in the face of warnings like "may kill honeybees in substantial numbers" and "highly toxic to aquatic and estuarine invertebrates," I don't remember. But, clothed in long sleeves, waiting for a still moment, and holding my breath to avoid being poisoned myself, I sprayed. Fortunately, it rained, requiring me to think about repeating the process before the unpleasantness of the first experience had worn off, and I decided that unblemished buds came at too high a price. I found less antisocial ways to deal with Japanese beetles.

One way is just to turn the garden over to them around the Fourth of July and reclaim it around Labor Day. Leaves get lacy and petals devoured, but on the whole, beetles like the garden when the air is hot and heavy and I don't, so giving them the dog days of summer isn't such a bad bargain.

If they are devouring things you really care about, and can reach, you can knock them into a jar of kerosene. Do it in the early morning and late afternoon when they are slow. This regimen requires perseverance and a kind of single-mindedness I don't have. I do, however, physically knock Japanese beetles off whatever I see them feeding on, because I have heard that even this temporary disturbance makes the garden less inviting to them because they are sociable and don't like having their gatherings disturbed.

I also destroy the fat, white Japanese beetle grubs when I see them in the soil. This process involving the thumb and forefinger is too gruesome to describe, but I would remind anyone who thinks this brutish that there is more honor in meeting the enemy face to face than there is in killing him at a distance with poison.

A more popular method of dealing with Japanese beetles is trapping the adult beetles in one of those ubiquitous green and yellow wind-sock-like contraptions that attracts them with floral lures and pheromones (sexual scents).

"I put my traps out on Saturday and by Thursday I'd trapped thousands," said Hanover Master Gardener John Deacon when I asked him how his trap was working. He also said anyone who thinks Japanese beetle traps don't work is crazy, which is why the title of this essay is not "Why Japanese Beetle Traps Don't Work." To say Japanese beetle traps don't work is to pick a fight with every gardener who uses one. And a trap full of beetles is hard to argue with. Simple arithmetic seems to suggest that if I have two beetles on the roses and I take away two beetles in a trap, there are no beetles left to eat the roses. But simple arithmetic doesn't mean much in the insect world. In the insect world, there are zillions of Japanese beetles, and if you take away a bunch, there are still zillions left to eat the roses.

"There is a flaw in assuming that because you are capturing a lot of insects in a trap, the trap is working," wrote Roger Swain for *Horticulture*. "For unlike the fur trapper, who is making a living from what is in the trap, the gardener is more interested in what is in the garden. Unless an insect trap is reducing the number of insects attacking the plants, it isn't working no matter how quickly it fills up."

Virginia Tech Extension Specialist Diane Relf agrees. In *The Virginia Gardener* she writes: "Although several Japanese beetle traps are on the market which are effective at attracting beetles, use of these traps has not been shown to be effective in preventing Japanese beetle injury to garden plants, since the traps attract beetles from a wide area."

Still, if John Deacon says the Japanese beetles where eating his canna lilies before he put up his Japanese beetle trap and they're not eating his cannas now, the traps are obviously working for him. My experience has been more like that described by Swain. When I used the traps, I had beetles both in the traps and on the roses.

The best solution to Japanese beetles I have known all along, but it took me until this summer to use it. I'll describe the solution in a minute, but first the two reasons I decided to do battle. First, I was concerned about the number of grubs in the lawn. Japanese beetle grub population densities in favorable sites can exceed 500 grubs per square yard, and at that level they can reportedly consume more plant tissue than grazing livestock. At densities of 5 per square foot, they can be a problem for turf grass, and although I didn't have that many, it seemed that in March there was nowhere I could dig without encountering more than I felt comfortable with.

I was also growing a wild Virginia rose, *Rosa virginiana*, that happens to bloom at the minute the Japanese beetles emerge. Yes, its fall foliage is nice and it has nice red stems in winter, but I began to wish I could get just a peek at its pink blooms before the Japanese beetles devoured them. So, I took action—this time responsible action.

I've just finished dishing out the organic solution to Japanese beetles, Milky Spore Powder. It's a substance composed of ground-up grubs infected with a common spore called Milky Disease, and it kills Japanese beetle grubs in the soil. Once established, it's almost 100 percent effective, and it lasts indefinitely. The spore dust comes in cans available at hardware and feed stores. It is most effective if everyone in the neighborhood uses it; otherwise, Japanese beetles can still invade from neighboring yards. But I have applied it in the hope of becoming one of many Beetle-Free Zones in Hanover.

Because it's so safe and effective, you would think gardeners would be waiting in line to buy this miracle cure, but it's expensive, a pain to apply, and takes a long time to become effective. A 20-ounce can, which will treat an area of 5,000 square feet, costs about $20. To apply it, you dish it out one teaspoonful at a time in spots 4 feet apart in every direction. It can go down at any time of year but should be watered immediately to help the spores enter the ground. The more grubs you have, the faster it spreads, but it usually takes about three years to become effective.

That's a long time to wait when the beetles are munching on your roses, but it's a short time if your real goal is no more war.

August

Learning to Live with Walnuts

As I walk across our lawn littered with walnut twigs, leaves, and fruit, I remember the time I was perishing to plant walnut trees. I was under the impression it took three generations for a walnut to bear fruit and that people who planted walnuts were creating a legacy for their grandchildren. If my grandchildren were to inherit such a legacy, I would need to start some walnut seedlings soon.

Now I'm glad the urge to plant walnut seedlings passed because I am having enough trouble with the one I inherited in the yard.

Don't get me wrong. I still love the *idea* of walnuts. Although I know now that it doesn't take three generations for them to bear fruit (it takes about 20 years), I still enjoy walnuts in the landscape, especially when they're silhouetted leafless against the sky holding their round fruits aloft. I still appreciate them, too, for their value as legacy trees since their lumber is truly valuable only after they are about 70 years old.

But a walnut is a tricky thing to deal with around a garden. Not only do the trees leaf out late and drop their leaves early, but their roots exude a toxic substance that inhibits the growth of some other plants. The substance is called *juglone*, and it has been found to kill American hollies, apple trees, azaleas, blueberries, laurel, potatoes, rhododendrons, and tomatoes.

Strangely enough, though, it's not toxic to everything. Walnut roots are said to have a beneficial effect on some plants. Researchers have found that certain forage crops like timothy, fescue, clovers, and mints actually thrive in the root zone of walnuts, although they aren't sure whether that is due to the presence of juglone or to the fact that walnut root systems increase the pH of the soil. I once read an article in *Country Journal* that advised planting black walnuts around the borders of a poor pasture to improve the pasture's quality.

Ah, that my black walnut could be put out to pasture somewhere where it could benefit some deserving forage crop instead of littering my cringing forget-me-nots!

Or are they cringing? That's what I would really like to know. For years I've saved every article I've come across that mentions which plants do and don't do well in a walnut's root zone. Much of the evidence is anecdotal—and some of it is contradictory; I found hemlock on both lists—but it helps in deciding what plants to try near a walnut. Interestingly, my list of plants that will reportedly grow under walnuts is now so long it begins to make a walnut sound like the Mother Teresa of trees, but that's just because I've been collecting examples so long. Here is the list of the plants and trees reported to do well within the root zone of a walnut: annual dianthus, astilbe, bee balm, beech, bleeding heart, campanula, clematis, cleome, coneflower, daisy, daylily, epimedium, euonymous, ferns, flowering dogwood, forsythia, four o'clocks, German iris, golden rain tree, hardy geranium, hawthorn, heuchera, hosta, Japanese maple, lamb's ears, lavender, lilac, monarda, periwinkle, privet, raspberries, rose, rose of Sharon, sedum, Siberian iris, Solomon's seal, spiderwort, spirea, sundrops, sweet woodruff, Tartarian honeysuckle, trillium, violets, Virginia creeper, wisteria, and "various spring bulbs."

In addition to azalea, rhododendron, and other plants listed earlier, plants that juglone is reportedly fatal to include wild columbine, Asian hybrid lilies, Baptisia, *Viburnum plicatum*, and mugo pine. Evidently, if you happen to see a plant like a rhododendron surviving under a black walnut it's not because the rhododendron has developed some sort of immunity to the toxin but because some barrier like a rock formation is shielding the plant's roots from the walnut's roots. Bacteria in well-drained soil also reportedly break down juglone, so walnuts growing on well-drained soil are supposedly less lethal to the plants growing beneath them than are walnuts grown on heavy soils.

In my own yard, impatiens, Italian arum, Jack-in-the-pulpit, Lenten roses, mock orange, Oregon grape holly, peonies, redbud, snakeroot, Tartarian asters, wild roses, and, yes, forget-me-nots, do fine within the root zone of a walnut, and boxwood seem to be doing fine under walnuts in my neighbor's yard. But are these plants really happy or just sticking it out? The answer is important because it would help me know how to deal with all the walnut litter falling on top of them.

In an article by an estate manager from Charlottesville, Virginia, I once read that juglone is in the bark, leaves, and fruit of the walnut, and that a 15-year-old rhododendron was once killed in a few weeks when mulched with black walnut husks. I have a faint memory, too, of once being told to keep walnut litter out of the compost heap because of its toxic properties. But just how toxic is this stuff? Are walnut twigs like hot ashes on top of my forget-me-nots? Are a few leaves in the compost heap a problem? How about a rakeful all tangled up with creeping Charlie?

It's a puzzle, and one that I would just as soon not have to deal with. The gardener in me says "cut the tree down"; the tree lover says "don't you dare." At the moment my husband sides with the tree, so it stands.

Besides, what would August be without running over walnut fruit with the lawn mower and raking up walnut litter? What indeed.

Nasturtiums: I'll Take Mine on a Green Plate

Ho, hum. There's a nasturtium in my salad.

Used to be you could wake up a family instantly by throwing a few nasturtium leaves in a salad. Then it took buds, and now it takes whole flowers to get anybody's attention.

Such is the popularity of edible flowers that now it takes new uses of old-standbys like nasturtiums to get flower-wise diners to take notice.

Just such a new use is what I came across recently in the June issue of *Mid-Atlantic Country*. In an article called "The Flavor of Flowers" there was a picture of red nasturtium flowers stuffed with something green sitting on what looked like white cheese served on a beautiful green plate. I had the flowers and I had the green plate, so I figured this was a recipe I could use.

That recipe turned out to be more complicated than I thought. What looked like white cheese was really jicama, a Mexican root crop that's a bit like a Jerusalem artichoke. And the filling in the nasturtium blossoms was a combination of mashed avocado, chopped tomato, chopped onion, garlic, and jalapeño pepper. I made the dish and have survived to say the result will really wake up a crowd, but, in the future, I wouldn't drive 20 miles to find a grocery store that carries jicama.

Beaverdam caterer Jenny Smith tells me she uses a cake decorator to fill nasturtium blossoms with a cream cheese mixture, and I bet the filling my neighbor Rosanne Shalf uses for squash blossoms—ricotta cheese, basil, and onion—would be equally delicious in nasturtium blossoms. The point is just to find a way to bring these colorful blossoms to the table, because if taste is as much a matter of the eye as the mouth, these vibrant flowers will wake any appetite.

All parts of the nasturtium are edible, and the small, round, lilypad-like leaves are full of vitamin C. Sailors used to take jars of pickled nasturtium seeds to sea to help ward off scurvy, and the green seeds are still used like capers in some recipes. One of the plant's common names is Indian cress because the plant's hot, peppery taste is a little like water cress.

Nasturtiums are old-fashioned flowers that I associate with marigolds and zinnias because they are easy to grow from seed and bloom profusely in cutting gardens of summer annuals and in vegetable gardens. Less often do you see them in carefully planned beds, but I read an article a few years ago that said that is just because most people don't know they can buy nasturtiums in anything but packets of mixed colors like yellow, red, and orange. Garden writer Christopher Reed described gardens in which nasturtiums of separate colors were used in sophisticated mixed borders. English gardener Gertrude Jekyll, for example, grew orange nasturtiums with marigolds and calendulas, and Christopher Lloyd has grown yellow nasturtiums in front of white Japanese anemones whose yellow centers the nasturtiums echo. According to Reed, nasturtiums should be more highly valued in the border because they are "weavers"; they crawl up into neighboring plants and stitch the border together with their blooms.

In August, it's hard to find nasturtium seeds in local stores, but you can still order them from seed catalogs. It sometimes takes as long as six weeks for them to bloom, but if you plant them promptly, there is still time to have flowers before frost. One company that offers packets of separate colors is Thompson & Morgan.

In addition to their value in the border and on the dining table, nasturtiums make great cut flowers. Their stems are delicate (you'd never jam one into a block of oasis), but you can put a few stems directly into a little vase of water or use a florist's tube to add them to a larger arrangement. Last weekend, in a room full of about 20 buckets of wedding flowers, a fellow arranger and I considered going back home for more nasturtiums when we realized the eight stems we had were more valuable to us than whole buckets of roses.

Nasturtiums are famous for being easy to grow, but I don't think they are fool-proof. Certainly, the seeds are great. Anyone who knows the sinking feeling of tearing into a seed packet only to find the promised 200 seeds taking up only ¹⁄₁₆ inch in the corner of the packet, will celebrate the size of a nasturtium seed. Not only are they fat—about ¼ inch in diameter—they are corrugated for easy handling! They should be planted about an inch deep because they require darkness for germination.

Beyond that, gardeners disagree about how to grow them. The conventional wisdom is that they are drought-tolerant sun lovers that do best in poor soil. Soil too rich in nitrogen will reportedly result in lots of foliage and not many flowers. But I have had more success growing nasturtiums in part shade than in full sun (one gardener tells me yellow nasturtiums can withstand the severity of the sun better than the crimson ones), and I think they need more water than they're usually described as needing. Certainly they need consistent moisture to get them off to a good start.

Finally, watch the variety you choose. The best ones for edging the border are the dwarf (to 15 inch) Jewel series cultivars and the even smaller Whirlybird series cultivars. The best ones for "weaving" or for growing on a trellis or fence are those that trail. Gleam series cultivars have semi-double flowers and will trail 2 to 3 feet, and the old-fashioned single-flowered nasturtium will send out runners that trail or climb 6 to 8 feet.

Nasturtiums bloom until fall, when you can take stem cuttings of your favorites, root them, and grow them on a sunny windowsill. Make it a kitchen windowsill, close to the cabinet with the green plates.

British Soldiers Hot on the Heels of Naked Ladies

Resurrection lily, magic lily, autumn amaryllis, and naked ladies—all these are common names for *Lycoris squamigera*, pale pink, lily-like flowers that seem to appear from nowhere on tall, naked stems in mid to late summer. Hot on their heels, blooming in late summer or early fall, are British soldiers (*Lycoris radiata*). British soldiers also bloom on leafless stems, but they have reddish flowers with wildly protruding pistils and stamens that give the flowers a spidery look and suggest the plant's other common name, spider lilies.

What odd plants these *Lycoris* are. I suppose there are some gardeners who can focus only on the four to six graceful, trumpet-shaped flowers that perch atop the 2½- to 3-foot leafless stems of *Lycoris squamigera*, but like an American gawker on a European nude beach, I can't keep my eyes off those naked stems. Naked ladies' bright green stems are as big around as my index finger and unusually straight and smooth. They grow from bulbs that send up broad, straplike foliage 12 to 18 inches tall in early spring, but by the time the flowering stems emerge in late July or August, this foliage has withered away. Seemingly overnight—like magic—the pale pink flowers appear, and many a gardener has returned from a week-long summer vacation to find a patch of blooming pink flowers where a bare spot had been when he left. Not only do naked ladies magically materialize in the garden, they pop up unexpectedly in lawns, a single flower rising like a mermaid in a sea of grass.

Where do these isolated naked ladies come from? I asked bulb expert Brent Heath that question because it seemed a mystery to me how these flowers could pop up in such unexpected places. A crocus out of place is easy enough to explain, because squirrels plant them where they want them, but *Lycoris squamigera* bulbs are enormous—turnip-sized—and they are poisonous, so squirrels wouldn't want them even if they could carry them.

"Are they seeding in?" I asked Heath, thinking this must be the way they moved.

"I suppose so," said Heath, although he said he's never seen *Lycoris squamigera* set seed and *Lycoris radiata* is supposed to be sterile. Another possibility is that the lawn in which a naked lady emerges wasn't always lawn—maybe it was garden when a previous owner planted the bulb. "Or maybe bulb fairies plant them," teased Heath.

Spider lilies or British soldiers are as eye-catching as naked ladies. Their naked stems are shorter than those of naked ladies (12 to 18 inches as opposed to 2½ to 3 feet), but their flowers are even more outlandish. Atop *Lycoris radiata*'s naked stems sit 8 to 12 reddish flowers, and each one, facing outward in a circular arrangement, has a long pistil and extremely long stamens protruding from it.

"As a child," recalls garden writer Allen Lacy, "I thought these circles of red spider lilies, which aren't lilies at all but members of the Amaryllis family, looked like merry-go-rounds." Perhaps the flowers suggested British soldiers to whoever coined that name for them because of their reddish color (think Red Coats) or because their stems stand so straight (at attention). The red-capped lichen we also call "British soldiers" is obviously unrelated.

Although both species of *Lycoris* have been perfectly hardy for me in Ashland, some books list British soldiers as hardy only to zone 8, south of our zone 7. Allen Lacy says Richmond, or possibly Washington, D.C., is as far north as British soldiers will grow, unless you lift them for the winter. Naked ladies, on the other hand, are hardy as far north as New England.

Both bulbs are available from bulb catalogs, but they are shipped only at certain times. Locally grown *Lycoris radiata* is shipped in June; imported *Lycoris radiata*, which comes from Taiwan, is shipped in September. *Lycoris squamigera* (Naked Ladies) are usually shipped in September and will bloom the following July. You can also beg bulbs from other gardeners because, like daffodils, they produce small bulbs around the large ones, and they can be divided after the foliage has died down. Both bulbs like full sun or light shade.

The real challenge in placing these bulbs, however, lies in finding a place for them where not just their flowering stage but their foliage stage looks comfortable. I still haven't quite figured this out. Even if you find a spot where the flowers look comfortable, sometimes the foliage looks out of place when it appears. So far, all I know for sure is that I like British soldiers massed in regiments rather than standing around like sentries, and that this plant's russet flowers are particularly dramatic planted where the late afternoon sun can shine through them and light them up. Placing naked ladies is even more of a challenge, because one wonders whether to try to hide their tall, naked stems or to flaunt them. You can clothe a naked lady by surrounding her with perennials—that way she takes on the look of a respectable lily—but for a garden that's as playful as it is pretty, I recommend leaving a few of them standing around in the buff.

Love of Shade Deepens with Age

I once read that the older a gardener gets, the more likely he is to grow hosta. I wondered what the connection could be until the author explained that as a gardener grows older, so do the trees and shrubs he has planted and his yard inevitably grows shadier. The shadier the yard, the more likely the gardener is to grow shade-loving hosta.

Whatever it says about age and shade, I find myself growing more and more hosta. In fact, plants that prefer shade to sun get the bulk of my attention now because most of the sunny spots in my yard filled up long ago. Now it's time to see what will grow under an elm.

Trial and error is the theme of my shade gardening. I know

better than to try growing portulaca in the deep shade of a Norway maple, but I'm still learning what grows best in which kinds of shade. Sometimes a plant that thrives in high shade where there is "bright light" and good air circulation will languish in deep shade where there is little light and poor air circulation. Another plant might thrive without any direct sun on the north side of the house, but it won't grow in an equally shady spot under a tree where it has to compete with tree roots. Only you know the exact configuration of the shade in your yard (where is the shadow of the tool shed after 3 : 00 P.M.?), and only you can find the appropriate plant for that spot.

Often it is not lack of light but competition from roots that limits the plants that will succeed under a tree. Maple, beech, and elm roots are particularly shallow and rob the soil of surface moisture. Mounding soil over the roots is not usually good for the tree since tree roots need air and too much soil can suffocate them. But, to give plants a chance to establish themselves under trees, I have occasionally mounded a couple of inches of light, porous soil over roots without noticeable harm to the tree. (See "Arboreal Acupuncture Helps Trees Survive" on how fill affects tree roots.) Eventually, of course, the tree roots will make their way back to the surface. To compensate for moisture lost to tree roots, you can provide extra water and add compost and leaf mold. Listen to your shovel, however, and if it says "I don't want to dig here," your azalea, or whatever you're planting, probably doesn't want to grow there either.

Because their roots are deeper, oaks make good "mother trees" and many plants will succeed under them that wouldn't under maples. Black walnuts, on the other hand, are notoriously bad parents. (See "Learning to Live with Walnuts.") Walnuts actually leach a toxic chemical into the soil that inhibits the growth of some plants that grow beneath them. The kind of litter a tree drops is another factor to think about when planting in their shade. Oak leaves, for example, are acidic and will benefit acid–loving plants like azaleas, rhododendrons, and hollies growing beneath them, but they are a mess falling into a tangle of winter jasmine.

What succeeds for me in shade may not succeed for you; "my shade" is a more meaningful term than "thin shade," "bright shade," "semi-shade," or "high shade." Here are some of the plants that have succeeded for me you might want to try: in moist shade, cardinal flower, cowslips, hosta, Jack-in-the-pulpit, Lenten roses, Ligularia, and lungwort do well. In dry shade, and even with competition from tree roots, columbine, epimedium, Lamiastrum, Lamium, money plant, and winter aconite, thrive. In woodland conditions (high shade where there's plenty of humus in the soil), wildflowers like American alumroot, black cohosh, celandine poppy, foamflower, Solomon's seal, white snakeroot, and woodland phlox do well. Hardy begonias spread like wildfire under the shade of my maples, but Bergenia and Brunnera, perennials that I have seen do well in other people's shade, languish in my shade, even where they don't have to compete with tree roots. In light shade, dwarf iris, spiderwort, Virginia bluebells, and wild geranium do well in my yard, as do old fashioned flowers like bleeding heart, forget-me-not, foxgloves, garden phlox, and lily of the valley. Even peonies can tolerate some shade.

In truth, the list of plants that enjoy shade is probably as long as the list of those that enjoy sun, but for some reason, we seem to be less aware of them. Could it be that awareness of shade-loving plants, like shade itself, deepens with age?

Big Trees from Small Seeds Grow— But How Fast?

Somewhere between the Scottish landowner who moved full-grown trees around his parks like bedding plants and the southern gardener who established a tree arboretum from seed are the rest of us trying to decide what size trees and shrubs to buy. Should I buy the

6-inch rhododendron for \$5 or the 4-foot rhododendron for \$50? Any gardener with an eye toward economy would lean (careen!) toward the \$5 rhododendron, but he should be advised that it may be three or four years before the smaller rhododendron blooms. Here are other things to consider.

If economy were all that counted, we would grow everything from seed. For example, the price of a pound of lilac seeds is \$33. We cannot assume they would all be viable, but at 90,000 seeds per pound, that's still tens of thousands of lilacs for \$33. Paper birch seeds seem relatively expensive at \$92 per pound until you realize there are an estimated 1,300,000 paper birch seeds in a pound. At those prices, and in nature, seeds are free, but, as a look at any gardener's checkbook will reveal, sometimes we are willing to pay someone else to shepherd our plants through their infancy.

Deciding what size trees and shrubs to buy usually involves balancing price with the growth rate of the plant, the needs of the garden, and the patience of the gardener. "How much is a year's growth worth?" is one of the first questions to ask yourself.

Let's say you want a tree to block your view of a telephone pole. You would like the pole to disappear as soon as possible, so you choose a fast-growing evergreen like a Norway spruce, which will grow 2 or 3 feet a year. If you go to the nursery and buy a 2-foot, container-grown Norway spruce, for example, it will cost about \$15. If you buy a 4-foot, container grown, Norway spruce, it will cost about \$35. Is a year's growth worth \$20 to you? That will depend on how ugly you find the telephone pole and how deep your pockets are. One of the beauties of gardening is that patience can always compensate for shallow pockets.

When I go to the nursery looking for trees and shrubs, I'm usually looking for the least expensive ones I can find, which usually means the smallest ones. "Got any small skip laurels?" is a question I've asked so many nurserymen so many times that some of them start counting their skip laurels when they see me coming. I want many of these expensive shrubs, and finding small, inexpensive ones allows me to create a rich man's landscape on a schoolteacher's budget.

Other than needing to block a view quickly, there are only three reasons I can think of for choosing large over small trees and shrubs. The first is that the scale of the garden demands it. The renovators of the gardens at Gunston Hall, for example, had to replace English boxwood in an established hedge. It wouldn't help to plant a tiny new one in the middle; it would never catch up with the established shrubs. Instead, the ladies of the Garden Club of Virginia trucked in boxwood so big and heavy that the bridges in Rockbridge County, Virginia, had to be shored up to get them across.

Large trees and shrubs are also sometimes required where traffic is a problem. If a tiny tree is going to be run over by the lawn mower or by children, a bigger tree is a better investment.

The third reason has to do with the psychology of the gardener. Sometimes we need a "quick fix"—an instant azalea bed or sizable new tree that seems to outsmart time and give us an established garden overnight. It's expensive, but sometimes it makes more sense to plant large trees and shrubs that make an instant splash than to plant small ones that are ignored, unwatered, and soon dead. No one forgets to water a $50 rhododendron.

But there are also arguments for planting small trees and shrubs. First of all, they are easier to establish. That Scottish landowner who moved full-grown trees around his parks boasted that he never lost a tree, but don't count on it, even if you can afford the labor of ten men for two weeks, as he could. As a rule, the bigger the tree, the harder it is to move, not just because of the physical labor involved but because of the shock to the tree's system. As Hugh Johnson reported (see "Plant

Trees—Don't Bury Them"), a small tree planted at half the size of a larger one will often catch up with and race ahead of the larger one in 15 years.

Starting small also allows you to buy more. You can buy ten $5 rhododendron for the price of that $50 big one.

But the best reason for starting trees and shrubs small is this: the pleasure derived from growing a plant is inversely proportional to the size it was when it was planted. That is, it's more fun to sit in the shade of a tree you started in a Dixie cup than it is to sit under one you hauled in on a flatbed truck.

"See that cherry tree," said my friend Philip Carroll, pointing to the cherry tree towering above him. "A neighbor of mine gave me that in a Dixie cup. I cut it down twice with the lawn mower. Now it's so tall I can't reach the cherries."

"See that weigela hedge," said the former owner of our house. "I ordered the shrubs as twigs from the one-cent sale on the back page of *Parade* magazine."

It's not the plants we've purchased at maturity but the twigs we've nurtured into trees that we gardeners are proudest of. And rightly so.

September

Welcome Autumn with Sweet Autumn Clematis

The clematis most gardeners are familiar with are clematis with 5- to 6-inch flowers that bloom in May and June, but it's a clematis with tiny, white, fragrant flowers that lights up backyards and perfumes neighborhoods in the fall. It's the sweet autumn clematis, and where allowed to run wild, it clambers over fences, drapes shrubs and arbors, and shades porches with thick tangles of smooth foliage topped with clusters of star-like flowers.

Common names for this vigorous vine include Virgin's

bower and Traveler's Joy, the names referring to the vine's ability to create a canopy so thick that travelers (and innocent maidens) can find shelter under it. In my neighborhood, there may be more canopies waiting to provide shelter than there are innocent maidens, because this vine runs rampant. I used to think it was *Clematis virginiana*, a native clematis with flowers almost identical to the ones in my yard, that was creating these canopies in Hanover, but I've recently learned that the clematis romping through my neighborhood is probably *Clematis dioscoreifolia*, a Korean species that has naturalized in many Virginia counties.* According to native plant specialist Dr. Dick Weaver, *C. virginiana* has 2- to 4-inch leaves with sharply toothed edges and *C. dioscoreifolia* has smaller, ovate leaves with smooth edges.

Both species have clusters of delicate, snow-white, 1-inch flowers, and both are fragrant, although sweet autumn clematis, *C. dioscoreifolia*, is reportedly the more fragrant of the two. Once enveloped by it, you'll find the fragrance of sweet autumn clematis as essential to late summer nights as the sound of katydids.

Autumn clematis's blooms last only a couple of weeks, but the long-lasting, seed-bearing structures that follow them prolong the vine's visual display. As these one-seeded fruits develop, they grow what look like white feathery tails, and plumy assemblages of them take on a hoary look that accounts for another of the plant's common names: Old Man's Beard. They not only provide food for birds but make great additions to wreaths and dried arrangements.

The vine has smooth, graceful stems but no tendrils and climbs by wrapping its leaf stalks around supporting structures or other plants. Evidently, you don't even need a slow-motion camera to see this. With his usual patience and keen powers of observation, Darwin once watched the process and described it

*You will also find autumn clematis listed as *C. maximowicziana* and *C. terniflora*.

124

in a notebook this way: "one [leaf stalk] revolved, describing a broad oval, in five hours, thirty minutes; and another in six hours, twelve minutes; they follow the course of the sun."

Because it grew on a little fence behind my family's home on Richmond's Van Buren Avenue, childhood memories alone would make me want to grow this sweet-smelling vine, but gardeners interested in creating memories should try it, too. Provided support, it grows easily to 10 feet (sometimes higher), and the most attractive use of it I ever saw was on the porch of Old Mansion in Bowling Green, Virginia, where Peter Larson had trained the vine to grow all the way around his doorway.

It will also grow up and over shrubs, providing a second show for spring bloomers like spirea, and it is gorgeous clambering up into evergreen trees like hollies and cedars. You must watch it, however, because there is a fine line between sweet autumn clematis that's adding another season's interest to a tree or shrub and sweet autumn clematis that's smothering its support. The vine can be aggressive and, once established, is harder to dig out than honeysuckle. Seedlings also pop up where you don't want them. One place where I've enjoyed sweet autumn clematis seedlings that planted themselves, however, is in a bed of English ivy where they have spread horizontally to cover the dark ivy, their sparkling white blooms lighting up an otherwise somber corner of the yard.

Sweet autumn clematis likes light, rich, moist soil, but if you provide it less favorable conditions (average soil, for example), you will have less trouble keeping it under control. It will grow in full sun or part shade and can be propagated by seeds, stem cuttings, or root division. New plants take time— they don't usually bloom until the second year—but once they are established, you will be wondering not how to grow them but how to prune them. Autumn clematis blooms on new growth, so you can prune the plants to within a few feet of the ground, or even to the ground, in late winter and still have tall vines loaded with clusters of white blooms by late summer. In fact, you can lightly prune the vines at almost any time without hurting them. I once had the bright idea of growing autumn clematis up and into a privet hedge, forgetting that I would be pruning the privet all summer and pruning the clematis, by default, at the same time. I cringed every time my pruners tore through that young, new clematis foliage when all they really wanted to do was whack that stubby, old privet foliage down, but the clematis recovered from even this untimely indignity and showered the privet hedge with blooms.

Collecting Seeds Turns Pennypinchers into Spendthrifts

If you're a seed saver, it's hard not to feel a sense of urgency in the fall when so many seeds are ripening. Will I be able to catch the cosmos seeds before they shatter? Living with a little harvest angst is a small price to pay for the rewards of saving seeds, however, because seed-saving allows even pennypinchers to be spendthrifts.

"Seeds are cheap," you say, "Why save them?" Sometimes seed-saving is essential because you have no other source for the seeds. Chinese temple bells, for example, is a beautiful hardy annual whose seeds I gather carefully because, with the exception of the gardener who first shared them with me, I know of no other source of the seeds. Many gardeners save seeds of heirloom vegetables for the same reason. Feeling as if we are saving money, albeit just a little bit, or outsmarting a seed company, is another reason for saving seeds. It is hard not to feel a little smug about a baggie holding thousands of bachelor's button seeds when you know you would pay $2 for 20.

But it's not the penny-pinching side of my personality that seed-saving appeals to—it's the spendthrift. I like to scatter seeds extravagantly, and for that you need seeds to burn.

One caveat about seed-saving: beware of hybrids. The seeds of hybrid plants are sometimes sterile, and even when they are fertile, they don't always grow up to look like the parent plant; they may look like one of its ancestors. Some people use "the hybrid problem" to discourage seed-saving altogether, but not all hybrids are sterile, not all hybrid ancestors are ugly, and not all plants are hybrids. The best advice I've heard on the subject of saving seeds of hybrids is not to depend on them but to experiment with them. Also, whether you're saving seed from hybrids or heirloom plants, experts recommend collecting seeds from more than one plant of each variety in order to maintain a broader gene base.

Saving seeds involves finding and recognizing the seeds, knowing when to harvest them, and knowing how to store them. Finding them is fun. Most everyone can recognize a marigold seed with its long, thin, black body and whitish feathered end, but what fun it is to discover that the envelope holding these arrow-like seeds actually looks like a quiver. Marigold seeds are easy to gather because there is usually enough spent petal material around the eveloping bracts to give you a fingerhold. Just pull the petal mush, and fifty or so seeds will come out with it. Wait until the seeds are mature, though. If the seeds aren't good and dark, or don't slide out easily, they may not have stored enough food to get them through the winter. Also, many marigolds are hybrids and will not come true from seed, but if you're not finicky about which marigolds you grow, you can enjoy letting them surprise you.

Cosmos is another ornamental with seeds you can gather at summer's end. After the flower petals have fallen off, cosmos seeds stand in a star-like arrangement. Just barely pinch the "star" where it joins the stem, and the seeds will tumble into your hand. Something I recently learned about cosmos is that darker colors dominate lighter colors in a cross, so if you want to keep light colors in your mix, better gather more seeds from plants with light petals than dark.

Zinnias are also supposed to be among the best flowering ornamentals to save for seed; like the other plants I've mentioned, they will sometimes even self-sow. I have a neighbor who grows a 15-foot row of zinnias every year from seeds he has saved every year for the past 15 after acquiring the origiinal seeds in a package one of his children brought home from McDonald's. But my one experiment with saving zinnia seeds wasn't successful. I was thrilled the day I started pulling dried petals away and found the zinnia's seeds in the flower's tight central core, but although I gathered oodles and planted them in a huge bed the following summer, only about eight plants came up. Were my parent plants hybrids with sterile seeds? I don't know. It is hard to tell bad seeds from bad culture.

At the other end of the spectrum was my experience with hyacinth beans. This ornamental bean with spikes of pea-like flowers and deep purple pods has great-looking seeds, black with a white stripe and about the size of lima beans. Once I figured out that the seeds weren't really mature until the pods looked grossly shrunken and misshapen, I was in business, because peeling back these rubbery pods yields seeds that are easy to handle and reliable to grow. I think every hyacinth bean I saved and planted came up, as did some that had self-sown, and I covered a 75-foot fence at no expense.

Calendulas are another ornamental with seeds that are easy to spot and collect. About the diameter of a pencil eraser, these ring-like seeds remind me of tiny coiled worms arranged in a rough circle around a center point. Although I've had no trouble catching these at the right moment (which can be as early as July or as late as October, depending on when you planted the parents), seed saver Marc Rogers warns that calendula seeds shatter quickly and can be harvested when immature if necessary.*

To harvest seeds at the right time you really need to inspect your plants every day, which is hard to do if you're working until dark or if you're gardening on a piece of land you don't visit

---

*This and other tips are found in Rogers's *Saving Seeds*.

every day. I was disappointed to arrive at my Buckingham County garden last weekend, for example, and see that all the pods on my spent arugula (salad rocket) plants had spilled their seeds. To bad, I thought; if I had collected them on time, I could have been planting them just about now. Then I noticed something green growing at the base of my spent arugula plants: a healthy new arugula crop. It seems sometimes a sense of urgency isn't necessary, and some ships come in without captains.

Fancy Packages Help Seeds Survive

First, I'll explain the importance of storing seeds dry, then I'll explain the real secret of successful seed-saving: fancy packages.

Seeds need to be dry when you store them for two reasons. First of all, many seeds need a period of dry storage in order to destroy the chemical inhibitors that keep them from germinating. This runs counter to what most of us think, that keeping seeds in a dry place prevents them from germinating. According to chemist Norman Deno, whose *Seed Germination Theory and Practice* describes the special germination requirements of more than 2,500 species of seeds, it's a common misconception that seeds will germinate if given a little moisture and a little warmth. "This misconception arises," writes Deno, "because seeds of many temperate zone plants can be collected, put in an envelope on the shelf, and germinated months later when given moisture and warmth. What is often overlooked is that the period of dry storage on the shelf was essential to the germination. What happens is that chemical inhibition systems are present initially and these are destroyed by the drying."

While not all seeds require dry storage (some require a cold, moist period to break their dormancy), the majority of the vegetable seeds we grow do. According to Deno, the reason so many of the crops we grow have seeds that require dry storage is that it was important for early man to be able to dry store seed over the winter and "what evolved in agriculture was an effi-cient selection for this type of seed." Most of our common an-nuals also require dry storage.

A second reason for storing seeds dry is that moisture can speed up the seed's metabolism, cause it to burn up stored food too fast, and reduce the seed's chances of successful germina-tion. So, as a first step toward successful seed storage, experts tell us to collect seeds dry. That sounds so easy but does nothing to explain the matted mass of mildewed seeds I found in my pocket the other day. When a friend is offering you seeds from her white cleome and it's raining, you take them wet. If you are forced to collect seeds wet, a fast way to dry them out is to spread them in the sun on old window screens, which allow air to circulate all around them, but if you don't have old win-dow screens, or your seeds are so small they'd fall through the mesh, you can dry seeds on paper towels, newspapers, or paper bags and "stir" them occasionally. Just make sure the wind isn't blowing or the surface too hot. Too rapid drying or dry-ing at too high a temperature, above 100°F, can adversely affect viability.

Even if the seeds you have collected *look* dry, experts say we should dry them further by spreading them out in an airy place on newspaper or paper towels for about a week. In the best of all possible worlds, you would turn them or change the paper under them a couple of times during that period. I must admit that when I've collected what I believe to be dry seed, I do nothing to dry them further before storing them, but I dare not tell you that always works; maybe I've just been lucky.

Dry seed will also reabsorb moisture from the air, so once they've been dried, seeds should be stored in a moisture-proof place immediately. What is a moisture-proof place? Well, the Taj Mahal of moisture-proof places would be something like a mayonnaise jar with silica gel, a desiccant, in the bottom. Into this jar you would place your paper envelopes of seeds and then screw on the top. Or you could mix seeds and silica gel in equal parts and store the mixture in a moisture-proof container. According to seed-saver Marc Rogers, exceptions to this are beans and peas, which should be stored in bags, not airtight containers.

I sometimes use pimento jars to store small seeds, and I have never bothered to add silica gel. I have also had success storing seeds in envelopes that are not airtight. The thing to remember about airtight containers is that if your seeds aren't really dry, you're going to be sealing moisture in with them, and that's bad. According to Rogers, damp seeds, stored in covered containers, deteriorate more quickly than dry ones in open storage. If you aren't going to be careful about drying, you're better off with your seeds in envelopes, where they can air dry, than you are with your seeds stored in mayonnaise jars, where they will rot.

Protecting seeds from heat is important, too. Although you will find most experts recommending that you store seeds at 40° to 50°F, Norman Deno found little difference in germination between seeds stored at 40°F and seeds stored at 70°F. That means you don't need to store seeds in the refrigerator, unless they're seeds that require a period of cold stratification, and we're not talking about those here. The refrigerator is, however, a safe place to protect seeds from mice, which explains why lettuce competes with seed packages for crisper-drawer space in my refrigerator in the country.

In Ashland, I keep my seeds in a basket on the utility room counter, and what a motley assortment it is: paper envelopes, plastic bags, film canisters, pimento jars, and yogurt containers, all filled with seeds. I do not recommend this messy system, because I think, all other things being equal, a seed in a pretty, properly labeled package has a better chance of survival than a seed in a scruffy sandwich bag.

The trick with saving seeds is to make them seem important, and nothing will do that better than a carefully labeled package or a picture. I estimate that a seed in a packet with a picture on it is about three times as likely to grow as a seed in a packet without a picture. Anything that bridges the gap between the size of the seed and the size of the hope and commitment required to make it grow will help. In lieu of a picture, give your seeds importance by including on or in their packages carefully penned notes about when the seed was collected, where it came from, or from whom. If you're in a hurry, you can throw a single, dry, recognizable flowerhead in with your seeds to serve as a label of sorts, but it won't inspire the confidence a proper label would.

I sometimes scotchtape labels to pimento jars and leave loose scraps of paper bearing notes in baggies of seeds, but what I really want are some of the 2- by 3½-inch and 3- by 5- inch manila envelopes you can write on that I have seen other gardeners use. The most delightful package of seeds I ever owned was sent to me by Manassas gardener Nancy Arrington who had labeled her tiny manila envelope not just with cultural instructions for wild petunias (*Ruellia ciliosa*) but with information about where and when she had collected the seeds. Like children whose parents are your friends, those seeds seemed destined to turn out well, and partially because of my confidence in them, they did.

Is Your Lawn an Ecolawn?

Stop. Hold that spreader, especially if your fertilizer has weed-killer in it. After reading this, you may decide to push on with your lawn care program, but here's an alternative to consider first.

How about an ecolawn? Researchers all over the country are working on lawn mixes that would be more environmentally friendly than the monocultures we currently maintain with fertilizers, weed-killers, and water. At Oregon State University, for example, blimps fly over test lawn plots photographing them to see which mixes are most pleasing to the eye. The desire to please the eye, especially our neighbors' eyes, is, after all, the driving force behind lawn maintenance. But these test plots at Oregon State are only 80 percent grass, and the grasses the researchers are growing are ones they have chosen because they *do not* thrive in the region.

It's true. According to Warren Schultz, author of *The Chemical-Free Lawn*, researchers at Oregon State and elsewhere are developing ecologically correct lawn mixes that typically include about 20 percent flower seed and 80 percent grass seed of a type that won't out-compete the flowers. In the northwest, for example, bentgrass would do too well and force out the flowers, so perennial rye is used instead of bentgrass in those mixes. Commercial companies are jumping on the bandwagon with mixes like Ecology Mix and Fleur de Lawn, and if your lawn currently looks like mine, a few of the flowers included in these mixes may be familiar. Strawberry clover, white Dutch clover, English daisies, Roman chamomile, and common yarrow are currently included in some mixes, and Tom Cook, a professor of turf science at Oregon State, is experimenting with including Johnny-jump-ups and two species of creeping violets in his eco-lawn mixes. Scientists at Harvard are proposing similar environmentally friendly lawns composed of plants adapted to the site that can be maintained with little effort. These "freedom lawns," as opposed to what they call industrial lawns, might include bluets, chickweed, crabgrass, dandelions, oat grass, plantains, quackgrass, sweet vernal grass, timothy, violets—all species that can tolerate mowing and can co-exist.

What I'm suggesting here is that you may already have the lawn that experts all over the country are trying to duplicate! And not only that, you are on the moral high road, because nearly everyone—except those in the lawn care industry—agrees that lawns are "ecological anachronisms." You know the problems: fertilizer runoff pollutes streams, lawn mowers pollute air, herbicides improperly applied kill wildlife, irrigation uses too much water. The statistics that most impress me are these: the American lawn is the largest crop in the world, using more fertilizer than all of India and Africa do. According to the National Gardening Association, U.S. households spend $6.4 billion annually on lawns. If you include all of North America and grassy areas like golf courses, industrial sites, and sports fields, we spend $25 billion annually on lawns.

I know these issues become complicated, particularly when there's no place you would rather spend money than your local garden-supply store and you know no one there wants to pollute the planet deliberately, but it does give one pause, considering other pressing problems, to think that we spend so much money growing fescue. In a visionary article about sustainable landscapes, Darrel Morrison of the University of Georgia School of Landscape Design described what a sustainable Piedmont landscape would be like in 2030 (*Georgia Landscape*, 1990). He predicted, for example, that expansive, resource-consuming lawns around homes and industries would be unfashionable, obsolete symbols of over-consumption and pretense. Alternatives to the expansive lawns, he said, would take several forms, each considered beautiful not only in response to the lines, forms, colors, and textures that are intrinsic to it, but also in response to its productivity and sustainability.

Sounds like ecolawns to me. So if you want to get ahead of the curve, think twice before working too hard to rid your lawn of crabgrass.

Avoid Rastafarian Roots   I have just graduated from root school and have a shed full of black plastic pots to prove it. Every root problem known to horticulture I encountered in a recent project that involved planting scores of container-grown shrubs. If you want to graduate higher in your class than I did, here are problems to avoid.

First, remember it's what's in the pot that's crucial to your plant's health, not just what you see above the soil line. Roots are to plants as the engine is to a car, and with poor ones you have bought a clunker. Unfortunately, the problem will not show up immediately. What will happen is that just as those treasured shrubs you planted years ago begin to fill in and really look like an established hedge, a plant or two may begin to lose vigor. The problem? A girdling root that started its spiral in the nursery and will continue, unless corrected, until it has strangled the plant.

In addition to circling or girdling roots, defects like kinked roots (roots twisted at sharp, abnormal angles), and J-hooked roots (roots sharply bent to one side), can also result in a tree or shrub that is poorly anchored or unable to absorb water and nutrients properly. What I have come to think of as "Rastafarian roots" are particularly problematic when it comes to water absorption. In the same way that hair will form a matted dreadlock if it continues to grow while tightly braided, roots will continue to grow in a pot too small for them, and they sometimes form an impenetrable mat of roots at the top of the pot where all those little pellets of fertilizer are. Rastafarian hair may be stylish, but Rastafarian roots are deadly. Avoid them.

Look at the roots of any container-grown plant before you buy it. I know that's easier said than done. A previously nice guy at our local Southern States feed store and nursery turned disagreeable when I asked him to pull a prickly, 50-pound Foster's holly from its container so I could inspect its roots. (If I could have, I would have done it myself.) When he groused, I capitulated, and, as a result, I ended up with a $60 plant that was horribly pot-bound.

A pot-bound plant is one that has been grown too long in a pot too small for it. What happens when a plant has outgrown its container is that its roots begin to circle and sometimes even grow back up into the root ball. A few circling roots at the bottom of the container or on the outside surface of the root system you can tease away with your fingers or a screw driver and spread into the surrounding soil when you plant the shrub, but seriously matted roots or roots that have headed back up into the root ball are harder to correct. Some gardeners routinely cut about an inch of roots off the bottom of a matted root system. Butterflying is another technique for correcting problems with severely compacted or circling roots. This involves first making four equally spaced cuts with a knife down the sides of the root ball, then making two crossing cuts through the bottom third to half of the root mass. These sections are then splayed (pulled apart from the bottom), creating four flaps which are then spread horizontally in the planting hole with soil placed around and over them.

But it is better to buy a plant with good roots than to have to correct for bad ones. White tips are a sign of good roots, as are small, supple roots. Avoid plants with roots that have black tips because they indicate rot, and avoid plants with large, rigid, circling roots. As I discovered last week, even small, white, supple roots aren't a sure sign you have a plant with a top-notch root system, however. At a local nursery, I had to talk a nursery-man into selling me some Russian arborvitae (*Microbiota decussata*) plants that he thought were too small to sell. "Let's look at the roots," I said boldly, and he obliged. They were beautiful—white, supple, and just barely filling the pot. I decided these were great plants at a great price, so I bought lots, thinking, "Oh, what a great plant shopper am I." It wasn't until I was home and shaking my plants from their pots that I noticed something funny. At the center of each plant was a tight Rastafarian core. Evidently, these plants had become root-bound in their previous pots, and although the roots that had ventured out into the soil of these bigger containers were healthy, the old matted core remained. Will the problem be terminal? Only time will tell, but suddenly some of the joy went out of the planting, because the plants' chances of survival seemed reduced.

In truth, I probably would have bought the plants even

knowing they had a root problem, because these were the only small, affordable *Microbiota* I could find. Unfortunately, that is too often the case: we wisely check our roots, discover them to be sub par, then buy the plant anyway. What choice do we have? It isn't as though they're expecting a new shipment of *Microbiota decussata* tomorrow at the 7-Eleven. Still, the more attention we gardeners pay to the roots of plants we buy, the more attention nurserymen will pay to the roots of plants they sell. At least that's what they taught me in the school I attended before root school.

Mowing like an Expert

On the subject of mowing, I am an expert. As chief groundskeeper at my Ashland home, I have spent more hours behind a lawn mower than some criminals have spent behind bars. I know every root, rock, curve, slope, hill, dip, and violet clump in the yard. I can even show you the exact spot on the front sidewalk were my mower has the best chance of starting. These things are not known to amateurs. Here, then, are tips from an expert on how best to mow the lawn.

First, good equipment is important. A lawn mower should be maneuverable; anything that sticks out on the side of the mower is going to be a hassle because it will find something to hit in its path. It should be light, or at least light enough to suit the operator. I have one lawn mower that mows the lawn in an hour, another that mows the same lawn in three. The difference, of course, is one of perception since one mower is so much heavier than the other.

A lawn mower also should have a grass-catcher, but not for catching grass. The myth that "grass clippings cause thatch" has largely been exploded, and we are now advised to leave light clippings on the lawn to decompose and enrich the soil. But you will want a leaf- or grass-catcher so that you can mow through leaves and collect their diced remains in the fall. This will cut raking time in half, if not eliminate it entirely, and the diced leaves can go in the compost heap where, if turned occasionally, they will decompose by spring.

Last but not least, the mower should be easy to start. The Rolls Royce of lawn mowers is no better than a Chevy if it won't start. My own lawn mower starts on the first pull almost every time, and I would recommend it to everyone except that the same mower, a model with a two-cycle engine, was the bane of my existence for years. No one could start it. The turn-around came with a new mechanic who accomplished in one visit what I had been trying to get done for years. Moral: if you have to buy a mower with any moving parts you don't understand—like a motor—be sure it comes with a good mechanic.

Your chances of starting a mower for the first time in the spring will improve if you run all the gas out in the fall and fill the tank in the spring with fresh gas, not gas that has been sitting around in the shed all winter. I've also heard that letting the mower sit in the sun a while before trying to start it helps.

Keeping the blade sharpened is important for a good cut, too. Researchers have found that a cut with a dull blade actually wounds the grass, saps strength, and reduces the grass's chances of survival in the summer. In other words, if you are cutting with a dull blade, you're torturing the grass. Have your blade sharpened in January so you won't have to wait in line in March.

Knowing when to mow is important, too. You want to mow no more than is necessary but often enough that you are never removing more than one third the height of the grass at one time. Different grasses have different ideal mowing heights, but for most fescues it's about 3 inches. That's pretty high and will probably require the highest setting on your mower. Don't buy a mower that won't go that high.

Does having tall grass mean you are going to have to mow more often? I say no, although this is an issue my husband and I never seem to agree on. To my eye, it's when the grass gets uneven that it looks as though it needs cutting, no matter how tall it is. I can get John to agree with me in theory, and I know he agrees it's better for the grass not to cut it down to a nub, but whenever he mows, the grass always seems suspiciously short.

Knowing what time of day to mow involves more subtle decisions. As far as the grass is concerned, you can cut it whenever it is dry. As far as the neighborhood is concerned, it's best to follow local traditions. In some neighborhoods, only heathens cut before noon on Sunday; in others, you can cut any time of day as long as there wasn't a party the night before. My own neighborhood is fairly relaxed on the subject, but I'm still relieved when someone breaks the morning sound barrier by starting a lawn mower or chain saw before I do.

Finally, there is the question of who does the mowing. I like to mow the grass, and I expect my family to be forever in my debt for this peculiar trait. For families without such an eccentric, I have but one suggestion. It seems to me that the person who mows the grass should be the person who cares most about what it looks like. This is seldom a teenager, although my teenage daughter tells me you can nurture a teenager's interest in lawn maintenance by providing compensation, a walkman, and a pair of cutting shoes that will keep her "real" shoes from getting messed up.

I sort of like green shoes.

October

Fragrant Shrubs Perfume October Air

In the fall, so focused are our eyes on the spectacle of turning leaves, we almost forget our other senses, but the nose knows fall is for more than seeing. Two fall-blooming shrubs whose fragrant flowers deserve as much attention as the leaves of any red maple are gardenia and Osmanthus, the former a shrub with showy flowers but a frail constitution, the latter a shrub with a hardy constitution but inconspicuous flowers.

Osmanthus could, and should, grow in every Richmond garden big enough to accommodate it.* If one grows in your neighborhood, you have probably gotten a whiff of its perfume without knowing where it was coming from, because a 10-foot Osmanthus can be loaded with tiny white flowers without anyone ever seeing them under the shrub's holly-like leaves. Holly olive and false holly are other common names for this handsome evergreen shrub that will grow in full sun or part shade. Its lustrous, holly-like leaves differ from those of a real holly in being opposite each other on the stem rather than alternating. An older Osmanthus also displays a leaf form that's different from

---

* *Osmanthus heterophyllus* is hardy from zones 7 to 9.

the juvenile plant's: its leaves are often smooth edged rather than lined with prickles as are those of a younger shrub.

It is not unusual in an older neighborhood to encounter an Osmanthus 15 feet tall and to be literally engulfed by its fragrance. My nose is so keen on this fragrance, I can sniff out an Osmanthus from a distance and consider it something of a challenge to find the source of the sweet smell whenever I encounter it. One of the nicest places to grow Osmanthus is right up against the house outside a window where its fragrance can waft in, but Osmanthus also makes a great evergreen hedge. The upright-growing *Osmanthus heterophyllus* 'Gulftide' is particularly popular for hedges.

The other contender for best fall fragrance is gardenia. We think of gardenias as summer-blooming flowers, but many of the new cultivars are almost as flower laden in September and October as they are in June. With their shiny, dark green foliage, thrifty habit, and 3-inch flowers, they would be staples in almost every small garden but for the fact that they are not reliably hardy in our area (zone 7). The experience of Ginter Park gardener June Adams is typical: she had grown a gardenia to chest height on the south side of a greenhouse, when, one winter, it was killed to the ground. "It's coming back from the roots," says June, "but it's only about a foot tall now."

"One should clearly understand," writes Donald Wyman in his gardening encyclopedia, "that the Gardenia is not as hardy as the Camellia." A gardenia called 'Chuck Hayes' is one of the hardiest, but even it needs some winter protection in Richmond. Developed by Virginia Tech researchers in Virginia Beach, 'Chuck Hayes' was at first believed hardy enough to survive in western Virginia (zone 6), but it didn't turn out to be that cold tolerant.

"There's no gardenia hardier than a 'Chuck Hayes,'" says Jan Gills of Colesville Nursery, "but a gardenia is still a gardenia. You need to site it properly. Even in zone 7, gardenias need to be grown in protected places, such as alcoves where the house blocks the winter wind.

Or they can be taken inside for the winter. That is where Ashland gardener Ritchie Watson has housed his potted gardenia every year for the past 15. "I bring it in about the time of the first frost, then take it out again in mid-April," says Watson, whose south- and east-facing sunroom provides his gardenia plenty of light. "It doesn't bloom like one in the ground," he says, "but it has occasional blooms in the middle of winter and scattered blooms from March to June."

Watson does nothing to prepare his gardenia in a 14-inch pot for the transition from the garden to the house ("I should, but I don't," he says). Watson also gives his flourishing gardenia occasional coffee grounds to provide it the acidic conditions it enjoys, and he waters it regularly. The plant's leaves will tell you when the plant needs water, he says, because they look limp.

For gardenia lovers, whatever it takes to keep a gardenia happy is what they will do, because few flowers are as fragrant or as useful for corsages. People who don't like them usually either find their fragrance too strong ("It gives me a headache," a friend told me recently when I tried to pin a gardenia on her), or they object to the way the petals turn brown when bruised. The way to deal with an old gardenia flower, however, is to take it off your shoulder and put it on your gardening hat. A gardenia's fragrance lasts longer than its visual beauty, and you can enjoy its fragrance without looking at it when it's on your hat. If you're like me, you will forget it's there and find yourself wondering where the fragrance is coming from. What a treat to discover the source of that haunting fragrance is you!

Etch a Landscape Sketch—with Leaves

Before raking your leaves away, take a minute to look at the fresh perspective they provide on your landscape. If you have enough of them, they work as well as snow to cover the con-tours of borders completely and erase the locations of paths. If, like me, you have a hard time visualizing changes in your land-scape because of what is already there, a cover of leaves will provide you a clean slate. Not only that, but you can use your leaves almost like paint to draw new borders and paths where you want them and to experiment with different shapes. When I described the process to my daughter, she likened it to using an Etch-a-Sketch, one of those toy boxes that uses magnetic filings to draw pictures that can be erased just by tipping the box. When drawing with leaves you can change the contour of a border just by pushing leaves around, and that's easier than defining a border's edge by turning up dirt with a shovel. Also, there's little penalty in terms of labor lost if you change your mind.

For example, if your lawn is covered with leaves, try raking leaves off the grass only where you would like paths or open ar-eas. Do the areas where the leaves pile up at the side of these paths look like good places for borders? If they do, you may be able to decrease the size of your lawn and increase the size of your borders, reducing lawn maintenance and providing your-self more places for ornamentals. Sweeping leaves off the grass also allows you to see, in bold green, the pattern of grassy areas which we otherwise tend to treat as just what is left over after we have put in borders, hedges, and trees. In truth, lawn is a landscape element in itself, and like white space on the printed page, it is crucial to your design.

You can do with a rake what it would take weeks to do with a shovel. Path seem a little narrow? Open it up by pushing leaves to the left and right. Bulge in a border seem too pro-nounced? Reduce it by raking leaves away. The paths and edges you create will be temporary, but if you find them satisfying, it's easy enough to pull the leaves off, turn the grass up under them, then re-mulch with the leaves. You might even be able to smother the grass if you have enough leaves. What I'm doing is defining my borders with leaves then turning up the dirt just around the edges to hold the shapes I like. If grass comes up through the leaves, I'll turn it under in the spring.

One thing you will discover about this method is that if you put your borders in the right places, you can cut down significantly on the amount of raking you have to do. To me, raking leaves off green grass is fun, like opening the curtain to a beautiful view, but having to lift big piles of leaves and carry them long distances is work. Locate your paths and borders properly, and you can rake your leaves right into your borders.

It sounds too obvious to bear repeating, but leaves belong under trees, and nothing is more logical than a border that lets leaves stay where they belong. This was brought home to me in a wonderful way at the end of September when John and I were fretting over where to put borders on our Buckingham County property. I would stand up on the porch and tell him where to drive in stakes, then he'd stand up on the porch and tell me where to drive in stakes, but we were getting nowhere, because there was no real rationale for any of the shapes we were coming up with until I saw something that perfectly defined where the edge of the border should be. I dashed from the porch and started driving in stakes as fast as I could before the wind blew, because our red maple had dropped an apron of leaves that perfectly mirrored the shape of its canopy above. This border shape, literally sent from heaven, now seems as right for its spot as the tree that defined it.

So let your leaves fall where they may and see what they can show you about where borders and paths belong.

Moving Big Trees and Shrubs— Without a Locomotive

As my husband and I were moving a 12-foot Shoosmith juniper from one part of our yard to another recently, I was reminded of the way landscapers moved full-grown trees to the Planting Fields estate in New

York—they built a railroad to the property. But there is more to moving a big tree or shrub around than finding a way to carry its weight. This is a cautionary tale inspired by seeing the juniper my husband and I had just spent all day moving topple over after the soil around its roots became soggy. That's one way to learn the anchoring function of roots, but there are better ways. Here are some transplanting tips.

In the best of all possible worlds, you would prepare a large tree or shrub for transplanting by root-pruning it for two years before moving it. This helps the tree form a more compact root system and spreads the shock of root disturbance over a longer period of time. You need a good diagram to show you exactly how to do it (P. P. Pirone's *Tree Maintenance* has a great one), but essentially the process involves first marking off a circular area some distance from the trunk of the tree (about 5 inches for each inch of trunk diameter), excavating parts of this circumferential area each year (severing some existing roots), and refilling the trenches you've made with enriched soil to encourage fine root development. The process requires patience, and the gardeners who have it deserve fine trees.

Whether you have root-pruned or not, when moving a large tree or shrub, the more soil you move with the roots the better. According to Pirone, bare-root planting is mainly used for deciduous trees up to 2 inches in diameter planted in the fall or spring; larger deciduous trees, evergreens, and trees moved in the winter or summer should be dug with soil adhering to their roots.

Sounds easy, but it doesn't look easy when the person doing the digging has virtually disappeared under the root ball and is throwing dirt out of the hole like a badger. How big a root ball do you need? A rule of thumb is that your soil ball should be 9 to 12 inches in diameter for every inch of trunk diameter, although evergreens can make do with slightly smaller root balls, and the root ball doesn't need to be quite as deep as it is wide. The root ball for a tree 3½ to 4 inches in diameter should be about 38 inches in diameter and 23 inches deep. The real limiting factor with root balls, however, is not size but weight. Soil weighs about 110 pounds per cubic foot, so by my calculations, the root ball of the preceding tree would weigh about 410 pounds. Big load for a middle-aged badger.

Even if you could, you would want to avoid lifting the tree or shrub out of the hole by its trunk. It's better to get a burlap sling or tarp under it and lift it with that. Knowing that there was no way my husband and I were going to be able to lift our Shoosmith juniper with root ball out of its hole and carry it to its new hole 10 feet to the right, my stepfather, a retired engineer, suggested we dig a trench from one hole to the other and drag the tree along. Ingenious idea that seemed like too much work. Instead, we kept removing dirt from the roots until the tree was light enough to lift. Bad choice. Aside from the additional shock to the tree, removing dirt from the root ball was like removing weight from an anchor. By the time we had finished, we had an oceanliner anchored to a cork. As soon as I watered the tree, it started listing, and it would have gone down like the Andrea Doria had we not rescued it with stakes and guy wires.

A few days later I learned a local nurseryman had moved two enormous American boxwoods for a neighbor for $60 each. His men used shovels to dig the shrubs, wrapped the root balls in burlap, then lifted them using a crane on a tractor. When I called to ask his advice about what additional maintenance my Shoosmith juniper might need, he said that with big trees and shrubs it's essential to keep them well-watered for two full years after transplanting. He also added, "you know, I really did that job for your neighbor too cheap." I know.

Catch the Joy of Leaves

"Every leaf you catch this month will mean a happy month next year." Take that prediction to heart, and you will never experience fall in the same way again. Instead of grousing about leaves on the ground, you'll be desperately diving like a wide receiver for every leaf you can intercept between branch and earth. You'll be surprised: they're not easy to catch, but what you'll also discover is that fall isn't just a season (a noun); it's an action verb.

Leaves fall, and the best part of the show they put on in autumn is the action they take in air. Watch the float of a big Norway maple leaf, the pinwheel twirl of a sycamore leaf, the whoop-de-doo of an elm leaf caught in an updraft (sometimes leaves fall *up*!). What is the longest time you have ever seen a leaf stay airborne? Which leaf has the most spectacular flight pattern? Is there a difference between a leaf trickle and a shower? Leaf fall is a quick show, and it's hard to plan for, as in "Let's go see the leaves this weekend." Real fall—the verb— occurs at unexpected times, like when it rains or when the wind whips up. It can't be photographed, because anything that would stop its action is, by definition, not fall. So go out and catch the action.

Then begin the next best fall activity—making a leaf collection. Leaf collections should be made mandatory in every school at every grade level. A good leaf should be a substitute for money. I can't tell you how often I have asked a natural scientist of one kind or another how his interest in his discipline began and been told it began with a childhood butterfly, leaf, insect, or shell collection. Big tree expert Richard Salzer's interest in trees began when collecting leaves for an elementary school project. Mussel expert Richard Neves's interest in aquatic invertebrates began when collecting and trying to identify shells along Massachusetts beaches as a child. Some of my favorite descriptions to the magic of childhood collections appear in Russian novelist Vladimir Nabokov's autobiography, *Speak, Memory*, in which he describes the joy of collecting butterflies and leaves. Instead of collecting leaves and attending to their shapes, Nabokov's teacher had her students attend to the leaves' colors. Here is Nabokov's description: "Autumn carpeted the park with vari-colored leaves, and Miss Robertson showed us the beautiful device . . . of choosing on the ground and arranging on a big sheet of paper such maple leaves as would form an almost complete spectrum (minus the blue—a big disappointment!), green shading into lemon, lemon into orange, and so on through the reds to purples, purplish browns, reddish again and back through lemon to green (which was getting quite hard to find except as a part, a last brave edge)."

What a wonderful idea! I've been making color collections of my own, and, although they're not carefully keyed to the color wheel, spectacular things they are. Instead of arranging them on paper, as I walk, I arrange them like a hand of cards, slipping a yellow tulip poplar leaf in here, moving an amber hickory leaf over there. You would have thought I had been dealt the ace of spades last week when I added a dark maroon gum leaf to my hand and had to rearrange every other leaf to accommodate it!

Everyone has his own favorite trees for fall color, but here are my top four.

Red maple: Some have bright red leaves, others have orange, lemon yellow, or apricot leaves, and some have combinations of those colors with green edges like the ones Nabokov noticed.

Tupelo (black gum): Shiny tupelo leaves don't all turn color at once; a few turn red long before the others, and before the leaves of other trees turn. You can find a luminous red tupelo leaf on the ground as early as July.

Norway maple: My husband says he's an inch taller for having hung from a branch to help me reach one of these yellow-apricot leaves one fall weekend. When they're on the ground, I can collect more to dry in the microwave, because I know of no better natural source of this peachy color for dried wreaths. (To dry leaves in the microwave, collect dry leaves, sandwich them between paper towels, and dry them on the defrost setting.)

Sassafras: This may be my all-time favorite tree for fall color. What the sassafras lacks in size it makes up for in light green, yellow, apricot, and orange leaves. Plant a lavender-blue aster under a sassafras, position a shrub with a red berries nearby, and you have what I believe is *the* most beautiful combination of fall colors—lavender, red, and apricot.

Which brings me to planning gardens around leaves. I'll never forget seeing a southern garden in which the color of the impatiens under maple trees had been chosen to complement the color of the leaves that fell into them. This was a gardener who saw leaves as ornaments to be appreciated not as litter to be raked up. In Virginia, impatiens are sometimes ruined by frost before many of our best leaves fall, but late asters, anemones, chrysanthemums, and fall crocus can be planted to complement leaf color just as well. Whether on the tree, in the air, or on the ground, leaves can be just as rewarding as flowers. Watch them, catch them, collect them, and you'll have a happy month *this* year.

Arboreal Acupuncture Helps Trees Survive

It is a cool October Saturday, and John Hugo is out looking for a drill that we hope is going to help save the life of a tree. It's got to be a big drill—strong enough to drive a 3-inch auger through 18 inches of badly compacted clay soil. I hope he hurries, because whenever I wanted to put myself into a bad mood today, all I had to do was think about my big maple in Buckingham County gasping for breath beneath a suffocating layer of soil.

What we are about to attempt is vertical mulching which is a way of alleviating the effects of soil compaction. The problem I'm worried about was created when we moved lots of top soil from the river bottom up to the area around our cabin in Buckingham. Heavy equipment actually did the moving, and there's the problem. A bulldozer can be careful but it can't be light, and every time it ran over our already compacted clay soil, I felt as if it were running over me. Even the professionalism of the operator turned out to be a problem because there was one spot near a maple that, to get the grade right, he kept working and working. And then there was the rain. The only thing worse than putting weight on heavy clay soil is putting weight on wet heavy clay soil. But I'm obsessing again.

What I want to share is information that will help you avoid similar problems when you want to fill around an established tree. First thing to remember: no part of a tree is more vital to its health than its roots. "Out of sight, out of mind" is certainly true of tree roots, but damage to roots that we can't see kills trees. Where the roots are comes as a surprise to almost everyone who thinks of them as driving deep and extending no farther than the dripline. In fact, 70 to 90 percent of all tree roots are found in the upper 18 inches of soil, and the lateral spread of tree roots can go far beyond the edge of the crown. Research on fruit trees has shown that their roots spread 3 times the tree's height in sandy soils, 2 times in loam, and 1½ times in clay. Instead of the image of a tree's roots mirroring the shape of the tree in the earth, arborists say we should picture the image of a tree sitting on its roots as similar to a wine glass (the tree) sitting on a dinner plate (the roots). So there's a big area around any tree in which any filling or excavating you do is going to affect the tree's roots.

How much is it going to affect it is the big question. Can I fill just an inch or two in order to get some periwinkle going? Can I excavate just a few feet into the root zone to extend my brick patio? No one can say for sure because the extent of injury to the tree will depend on the species of tree, its age and condition, as well as factors like subsequent exposure to disease agents. If you're filling, the depth and type of fill is a big factor, too. Even an inch or two of clay fill can cause severe injury, but some experts say most trees can survive several inches of gravelly soil through which air and water can pass. Any time you put a blanket of soil around a tree you are disturbing the amount of water and air it receives, but some trees can take more disturbance than others. According to New York Botanical Garden plant pathologist P. P. Pirone in *Tree Maintenance*, the trees likely to suffer the most injury from fills are beech, dogwood, oak, pines, spruce, sugar maple, and tulip tree. Birch, hemlock, and hickory suffer less, he says, and elm, locust, pin oak, poplar, sycamore, and willow suffer least. Old trees, according to Pirone, are more sensitive to root smothering than young ones.

If heavy equipment is spreading your topsoil, you have an even bigger problem because the weight of the machinery compresses the soil, drives the air out of it, and makes it harder for roots to penetrate.

Vertical mulching, the arboreal equivalent of acupuncture, may help. It involves drilling holes 2 to 3 inches apart and 18 inches deep in the soil over the tree root zone and filling them with a porous material like sand, pea gravel, or perlite through which air and water can pass. Obviously, the drilling itself is going to cause some root damage, but the benefits of the procedure reportedly outweigh the risks. According to Pirone, although there is no scientific evidence to prove the procedure's benefits, arborists using the technique report improvement in tree health, and a landscaper I know insists it helps save trees.

I am more than willing to try it. Not only is there more new soil around our maple than I'd like, but I know the clay beneath it is more compacted now than it was before we began this project and it was pretty bad then. To anyone contemplating a soil-moving project around trees, I would say: remember it's easier to avoid compaction than it is to correct it. To my maple, I can only say, "hang in there, we're coming, we're coming."

It's Hard to Go Wrong with a Japanese Maple

The day my husband came home from the nursery with our Japanese maple, I was disappointed.

I thought I had given him perfect instructions about which kind to get, but I should have known that picking out a Japanese maple is at least as complicated as picking out black olives. Black olives are symbolic of all the things I've asked John to pick up for me on his way home from work only to discover that, although I think I've given him all the necessary information, like size and brand name, I've invariably left out a crucial category, like pitted or unpitted.

With the Japanese maple, the category I had forgotten was "Do its leaves stay red all year?" The specimen John had so lovingly picked out from the Little Five Azalea Farm was obviously one whose leaves would not stay red throughout the growing season, because they were already beginning to turn green, as the leaves of some Japanese maples do in the summer. At that time in my life, perfection was more important to me than peace, and I'm not proud to say I complained. In fact, it seems to me that I was grousing about what a shame it was to be planting a tree whose imperfection would grow more glaring every year even as we planted it.

That imperfect little sapling is now a handsome 20-foot tree, and I love it all the more because it doesn't have the boring habit of having its leaves stay red throughout the growing season. Instead, it warms up like a wood fire in the fall, and by Halloween it's as bright as a pumpkin.

If you are not familiar with Japanese maples, I should back up and say it's a wonderful tree to get to know. There are more than 250 cultivated varieties that vary in size, habit, leaf color, leaf shape, and even bark color, but the most common Japanese maple is a small- to medium-sized tree with an interesting layered branching pattern and palmately lobed leaves that are an unusually rich red.

What's so wonderful about these trees is not just how ornamental they are but how easy most of them are to grow. If we thought of Japanese maples as perennials that just get bigger and more beautiful every year with absolutely no effort on the part of the gardener after planting them, I think we'd see more of them planted in the landscape.

They like good soil and a moist but well-drained situation. Unlike many ornamental flowering trees, however, Japanese maples tolerate part shade, even prefer it in hot parts of the country, and they make perfect companions for dogwoods and other understory trees. The combination of a pink dogwood, a white dogwood, and a red-leaved Japanese maple can't be beat.

So: what kind do you want? Most landscapers prefer Japanese maples (*Acer palmatum*) with leaves that stay red, and you will pay for the privilege of having one. A hybrid like 'Bloodgood' has foliage that stays red throughout the growing season.

My Japanese maple, the one that started its life being blamed for being imperfect, is an unnamed variety. It was probably grown from seed rather than grafted as most of the more expensive, named varieties are. As I said, it has beautiful red leaves in the spring and fall, but they green out during the summer. That I once considered this a defect, I now find laughable. Maybe it's just that I've learned to love everything about my Japanese maple because we've grown up together, but I think I could make an objective case for a Japanese maple whose leaves change color being more dynamic than one whose leaves stay the same color throughout the growing season. I know I appreciate the red leaves of mine all the more because I know they're ephemeral. I even enjoy the difference between their spring red (a burgundy red) and their fall red (an orangey red).

I guess the upshot of all this is that it's hard to go wrong with a Japanese maple, which is more than I can say for olives.

November

November Loves Nandina

Some winters are hard on nandina, leaving her ragged and bare, but fall positively adores her. The pools of red that have been concentrated in the leaf nodes of nandina's glossy foliage all year seem to spill out in November, coloring the leaves and berries. The more sun this shrub gets the redder its foliage, but the berries are bright red even in partial shade.

Nandina domestica is the botanical name of this tough, adaptable shrub. Native to China and Japan, it's called *domestica* because of its association with the Japanese home, and the Chinese credit it with the ability to restore domestic happiness. According to Chinese folklore, when a dispute arises, if each married partner will tell his or her troubles to the nandina, harmony will be restored. For this reason alone, no American home should be without this shrub.

Fortunately, it's easy to grow. So easy, in fact that a landscaper who was recently hired to redo a job botched by another contractor told me that of the hundreds of shrubs that had been planted on the property, only the nandina survived the poor siting and improper planting. Although nandina likes moisture and leaf mold, it will grow in most any soil, in sun or shade.

The only thing hard about growing nandina is deciding how best to enjoy it. In the summer I want to cut its big trusses of small white flowers to use in arrangements, but if I do, I won't have berries in the fall. In the fall I want to cut the berries to use in the house, but if I do, I won't be able to enjoy them on the bush. I would also like to share the berries with the birds, but I'd like to have enough left over for myself. The only solution I see is to grow so much nandina you have plenty to go around. It's beautiful grown in groups or drifts, and in any shrub border it will soften the effect of coarser shrubs.

But if you don't have much nandina, and you really don't want the birds to get your berries before you can use them in Christmas arrangements, you can pick them in November and set them aside to dry. The stems will stiffen (an advantage since the overburdened stems want to flop in arrangements), and the berries will deepen in color. Although eventually the berries will get so dry they will start falling off, you'd be surprised how long these big panicles of berries last. I've had dried nandina berries last for years in wreaths.

The only real challenge in growing nandina is keeping it at the height you want and keeping it from looking naked around the bottom. I've had experts give me different advice about how to keep nandina bushy and compact. One nurseryman says to cut all the old canes back, each at a different height, in early spring. Another says to cut a third of the oldest canes to the ground each year after the shrub has reached the size you want. A third says, "Just cut back what you need to cut back in March; you could cut it to the ground and it wouldn't kill it." What to do with such advice? Sometimes I cut the leggiest canes to the ground in early spring—that's when I feel aggressive or my shrub looks particularly ragged; other times I cut the leggiest canes about two-thirds of the way to the ground. My nandinas aren't as bushy as some I've seen, but they're not standing around on bamboo legs either. Even when you cut the canes to the ground, you'll be amazed to see how quickly new growth comes up to cover the bottom of the shrub. Another way to deal with nandina's tendency to get bare at the bottom is to plant an apron of evergreen shrubs around it.

In addition to the 4- to 5-foot nandina most of us are familiar with, there are many cultivars, including a dwarf nandina that doesn't grow over 2 feet tall and a white-fruited variety called *Nandina domestica* 'Alba.' The latter's berries are really a dull yellow, and, although they may sound awful, I love to use them in Thanksgiving and Christmas arrangements. The foliage of *Nandina domestica* 'Alba' also differs from that of red-fruited nandinas in that there is no red in it. Recently this was the factor that made me choose *Nandina domestica* 'Alba' over a red-fruited nandina for a foundation planting where I didn't want red foliage competing with the yellow fall foliage of trumpet vine behind it.

A member of the Barberry family, nandina has yellowish wood and aromatic twigs that have been used as toothbrushes and toothpicks. One of its common names is heavenly bamboo, an allusion, I imagine, to both its bamboo-like stems and to the level of admiration this shrub enjoys.

These Camellias Brave the Cold

Imagine looking at a flower as elegant as a camellia and seeing your breath condense in the cold air around it. Such an experience sounds unusual, but it happens all the time if you grow sasanqua camellias. Sasanquas are the camellias that bloom in the fall. Try to remember the name "sasanqua," because it's the name that differentiates these camellias (*Camellia sasanqua*) from the more familiar *Camellia japonica*, which blooms in late winter and early spring.

Although their blooms and leaves are smaller than their spring-blooming relatives', fall-blooming camellias (sasanquas) make up for their smaller flower size by blooming when few other such refined flowers do. "Everything blooms in the spring," says Richmond nurseryman T. D. Watkins III. "Sasanquas are the way to go, because they bloom in a neglected season, and they're hardier than spring-blooming camellias."

Like spring-blooming camellias, sasanquas come in shades of pink, red, and white and they have single, semi-double, or double blooms. I like the single or semi-double ones; with their dense clusters of prominent yellow stamens, some of them remind me of miniaturized single peony blossoms, others of wild roses. Many of them are fragrant, and, although they don't last long, they are gorgeous in fall flower arrangements. Three of my favorites are 'Cleopatra,' which has single, rose-pink flowers, 'Hana Jiman,' which has single, white flowers tinged with pink, and 'Jean May,' which has shell-pink, semi-double blooms.

Even without blooms, sasanqua camellias would be valued by gardeners and arrangers, because the shrub's foliage is so handsome. Two to 3 inches long, the sasanqua camellia's evergreen leaves are a dark, glossy green and, on most sasanquas, they're held gracefully on the stem. I can remember rationing my sasanqua foliage when my shrubs were small (Do I dare cut another 6-inch twig?), and, even now that the shrubs are big, I cut their foliage judiciously because it is slow-growing and I value it so much for arrangements; in winter it's often the best-looking foliage around.

Although the growth habits of *Camellia sasanqua* varieties vary, they are generally more open in habit and more informal looking than the spring-blooming *Camellia japonica*. They're often used as focal points in mixed borders and in foundation plantings (or even espaliered on the side of a house) where they can benefit from the protection offered by the house. They're supposed to be hardy to zone 7, but even in zone 7 they benefit from protection. The best place for them is a spot where they are protected from the drying effects of sun, from abrupt temperature changes, from winter wind, and from the coldest temperatures. Where's that (other than in a conservatory)?

Well, of the four healthiest sasanqua camellias I am aware of in Ashland, two are on the north side of a house, one is on the south side of a house, and one is on the northeast side of a house. All of them share the protection of a house (think of the house as protecting the plant the way a person beside you at a football game protects you from wind and cold), and none of them is on the southwestern side. The latter I had thought must be significant but didn't know why until, in chatting with Watkins, he explained that fruit trees, and probably tender shrubs like camellias, gardenias, and daphne, get something called southwest injury when they're grown on a southwestern exposure. Such an exposure captures the heat of the late afternoon sun, and in winter this can result in dramatic and damaging temperature fluctuations when the sun drops below the horizon. According to Watkins, camellias shouldn't be planted where they receive bright sunlight first thing in the morning either.

Sasanqua camellias grow best in part shade, and they like moist, well-drained soil that's high in organic content. Container-grown plants can be planted in the fall, and because so many of them are blooming in nurseries, it's a good time to pick them out. Plant them "proud"—sitting high on the soil, not deep. They should be planted so that the soil line in their container is just even with or 1 inch above the surface of the surrounding soil. You can make up the difference with mulch. Because they are shallow rooted, deeper planting can smother them. Cultivating around them can also damage their shallow roots.

One of the best mulches for camellias is pine needles which allow air to reach the roots and acidify the soil as they break down.

Experts recommend fertilizing camellias as new growth begins in the spring by scattering a small amount of cottonseed meal or rhododendron-azalea-camellia food under the plants, but mine, lush and full of blooms on the north side of the house, have been fertilized only twice—once with fertilizer, once with compost—in the ten years since I planted them. Pruning is also a non-issue for me because a lanky camellia branch gets snipped off for flower arrangements before the thought of pruning ever enters my head, but should your sasanqua need shaping, you can prune it in early spring. Call a flower arranger and he or she will be glad to cart off your debris.

Two Tools Bridge the Muscle Gap

If you're a small gardener with big projects, here are two tools that will help you bridge the muscle gap. The first, and in my opinion most essential, is a mattock. The dictionary defines a mattock as "a digging and grubbing implement with features of a spade." Picture a tool like a pick ax with a 3-inch cutting edge on one side and a 2-inch cutting edge oriented in the other direction at the other end. It has a handle about 3 feet long, and it's a tool that you use standing up, as you would a hoe.

What is extraordinary about a mattock is the power it gives you. It's a heavy tool, but if you can lift it (and even a shrimp like me can), you can use it. I'm sure there is some physical law that says the work a gardener can do increases in direct proportion to the downward thrust of a mattock, because I have completed jobs I would have never considered possible without such a tool. Because it's so heavy, it can pierce right through a really big root. How big? On a good day, with more than one whack, I can dislodge a 3½-inch root. It's the only tool that has enabled me to grub out bamboo roots, and without it I'd be typing in a jungle right now. You would be amazed how easy it makes things like grubbing out privet roots that otherwise give new meaning to the word *tenacious*.

I use it for less onerous projects, too. If the ground is too hard to allow you to dig with a shovel, you can still crack it open with a mattock. Of course, if your ground is that hard,

159

you wouldn't do anything so inhumane (inherbane?) as to move a plant into it without amending the soil, but a mattock at least gives you a point of entry. Also, if you're digging a deep planting hole for a tree or shrub with a shovel and eventually reach subsoil, you can use the mattock to break up what is often hardpan at the bottom of the hole and vastly improve drainage under the plant. Occasionally, I've even used a mattock to trench the edge of a garden bed. All you have to do is lift it, let it drop, and you've sliced a 6-inch wedge out of the soil.

The other tool I'm hawking right now is a digging bar. It's not a gardening tool per se and it's not one that I have used, but my husband uses it all the time, and I was particularly impressed to see what he did with it last weekend. I had asked him to dig a hole for a birdhouse post and we couldn't find the posthole digger—another great tool, but if you share one with the entire neighborhood, as any posthole-digger owner should, you will never know where it is. I suggested digging the hole with a shovel, but John would have none of it. Instead, he went after his digging bar.

This tool he loves the way I love my mattock. It looks like a long iron bar but is made of tempered steel. It's about 5 feet long, 1½ inches in diameter, and weighs about 25 pounds. What John uses it for most is prying up stumps and putting in metal fence posts. With it, he has dug out stumps that I would have sworn would take a backhoe. The secret is leverage. John says you could lift a car with it if you had the proper fulcrum, because its heft is such that it just won't bend. To make a hole for one of those metal fence posts used to support wire fencing, all you do is lift the pry bar, drop it, let its tapered end slice into the soil, and push it back and forth. Do this straight up and down a couple of times and you've made a hole about 3 to 5 inches in diameter, and, if the soil is relatively loose, about 18 to 24 inches deep. It makes a nice tight passage for those thin metal posts, unlike the wider hole a posthole digger would make. Dislodging rocks is another good job for a digging bar.

Digging holes large enough in diameter to accommodate a

birdhouse post is not the work a digging bar is intended for, but it did the job. The job took some serious wiggling of the digging bar and some supplemental enlarging of the hole with a trowel, but it eventually made a hole that perfectly accommodated a cedar post about 6 inches in diameter which we sunk 3 feet in the ground.

A digging bar and a mattock cost about $25 each. Considering the work you can do with them that you can't do without them, that's a bargain, and cheaper by far than gym fees.

Don't Throw Shrub Covers Away

This is your last warning: I'm stealing your covers.

I'm referring to all those pine needles you're piling out by the street. I'm trying to stuff them all in the back of my station wagon before the town truck picks them up, but you're discarding them faster than I can get them. Why?

To my mind, pine needles make the best mulch, and it pains me to see a huge pile of them dutifully raked out to the street while naked shrubs stand shivering around the porch. Why not rake the pine needles under the shrubs?

Winter mulches protect shrubs from the ravages of weather by insulating them not only from the cold but from unseasonal warmth that would rouse them too early. Ideally, you wouldn't put a winter mulch on until the ground has frozen, but I think the danger of inviting animals to nest in a mulch you put down too early is less serious than the danger of waiting too long and not getting it down at all.

There are many qualities a good winter mulch should have, and pine needles have them all. First of all, they are cheap, or at least freely available if you have pine trees growing in the neighborhood. If you had to buy them, you would find they cost around $6 a bale. They're breathable, letting air circulate through and under them, whereas some heavier mulches smother plants. They decompose slowly, but when they do, they add organic material to the soil. They don't blow away, and they look beautiful.

The only strike against them is their acidity, which can be turned into an asset if you use them around acid-loving plants like hollies, azaleas, and rhododendrons. Just don't use them around lovers of sweet (alkaline) soil—plants like lilacs, clematis, and most herbs.

Thinking of pine needles as the down comforters of the plant world will make you less likely to discard them.

And if pine needles are the down comforters of the plant world, oak leaves are the wool blankets. They're not quite as attractive, but they get the job done. I swore last summer that I wouldn't rake any more of my fallen leaves into the street for the town crews to pick up because by July I always wish I had all that organic matter back. So this fall I did a better job than usual of shredding the leaves with the lawn mower and collecting them in the grass catcher, but a few were just too easy to rake out into the street. What surprised me, however, was how much their volume was reduced by shredding them. A mountain of leaves run through the mower becomes a basketful. Scattering them around shrubs and trees (acid-lovers, since oak leaves, too, are acidic) or adding them to the compost heap feels more generative than raking them away.

And evidently, this "feeling" is reality based. A study reported in *National Gardening* compared the nutrients in composted leaves to the nutrients in composted manure and found that the average humus pile contains twice the feeding elements of an old manure pile. Surprised? I was. According to researcher Florence Bliss, animals assimilate almost all the nutrient content in the vegetable matter they eat, leaving a bare minimum in the wastes they excrete. The microorganisms that recycle the organic matter in a humus pile, on the other hand, leave more food than they take out.

What this means to me is that it made no sense to drive 5 miles away to get horse manure from a friend on the same day

I had decided I didn't have time to pick up and move to the compost heap those leaves I raked out to the street.

If you are trying to make your yard wildlife friendly, you'll also want to leave some of your leaves and pine needles where they fall, because they create what one biologist calls "leaf litter feeders." Although some birds, notably robins and grackles, like feeding in grassy lawns, more birds prefer probing for food in leaf litter. The areas where we allow leaves to stay on the ground are usually moist and humus-rich, with an abundance of insects, worms and other invertebrates—a smorgasbord for birds.

What's a homeowner to do if he doesn't have a ready supply of leaves or pine needles? Stealing covers is obviously a crime I'm willing to commit, but if you don't have neighbors silly enough to leave their covers out by the street, you can buy mulch or go to the dump and see if you can find some there. More and more municipalities are composting garden refuse and offering it back to homeowners free. If the leaves and pine needles piled up in front of houses along Ashland's streets are any indication, however, most neighborhoods have plenty of blankets to go around, and none of our shrubs should face winter without being tucked in.

You Don't Have to Be a Chemist to Compost

On a recent tour of five world-class gardens, I saw immaculately groomed landscapes, borders brimming with priceless plants, and artistic hideaways graced with exotic statuary, but the phenomenon that impressed me most was Betty Lottimer's compost heap. "It will give you a compost high," said one of my fellow travelers as she pulled me over to see it.

To imagine Betty's compost heap, picture a pile about as wide and long as a queen-sized sheet and 3 to 4 feet tall. A shovel has made inroads into one edge of the pile, and this vertical surface allows you to see that, to its core, this pile is nothing but rich, moist, dark brown material that looks like premium potting soil. You can't resist touching it. Yes, it crumbles in your hand.

Although most gardeners know the value of compost in growing healthy plants, fewer gardeners know you don't have to be a chemist to make compost. Articles about balancing carbon and nitrogen ratios, adding bioactivators, and making layers of brown and green material tend to obscure the fact that anyone who is willing to wait long enough can make excellent compost just by throwing all his garden debris in the same place.

This is passive composting, which can take one to three years as opposed to active composting which produces compost in a matter of months. In order to achieve quick and efficient decomposition, active composting requires attention to carbon/nitrogen ratios and frequent aeration or turning of the pile; passive composting lets time do the work.

All you really need in order to create a passive compost heap, apart from garden debris, is space. You will need a space at least 3 by 3 feet on level ground, so your pile won't wash away. If you don't have available space because you have filled every corner of your yard with priceless perennials, take out some priceless perennials. A compost heap is that important. I once heard garden writer Jeff Ball say the compost heap would be the backyard shrine of the 1990s, but even if you're not ready to display your compost heap like a sundial, you can find a place for it. Hide it behind a screen of shrubs or build a fence around it.

Betty Lottimer's garden was clearly designed by a practicing gardener, because, far from being an afterthought, the location of the area in which she composts is both accessible and nearly invisible; it's in a corner of the garden screened from view by a high wooden wall. In one corner of this 12- by 12-foot enclosure is the pile she has let sit for two years, the pile that has now turned to black gold; in the other corner is the pile to which she is still adding debris—leaves, twigs, dead flowers, weeds, straw, grass clippings, kitchen scraps. The only kitchen scraps she doesn't add to her compost heap are meat scraps, which tend to break down slowly and attract unwanted animals. I make a little hole in my compost heap with my hand before emptying even vegetable kitchen scraps into it. Then I cover them with garden debris so as not to attract animals.

Here are other composting tips based on Betty's and others' experience:

Don't make your pile over 5 feet tall because air will be squeezed out and the material won't compost as fast.

The smaller the pieces of whatever material you put in your compost heap, the faster it becomes compost. Shredding leaves, for example, will help them decompose faster.

The materials in your pile should be moist but not wet. Some experts recommend covering your pile with a tarp to keep rain from soaking it and compressing it, because too much moisture and not enough air slows down the decomposition process, as does too little moisture. Even with no cover, your pile will decompose eventually, however.

Composting bins made of wood, chicken wire, cinder blocks, or other materials are dandy, but not necessary. Just a pile on the ground works fine, albeit slower. As Betty Lottimer's example proves, you don't even have to turn your pile if you choose not to; turning the pile just speeds the process. If you do want to turn your pile occasionally, as I do, you'll need either an empty bin beside your full one or a place on the ground into which you can turn your existing pile. A pitch fork works best for the turning.

If your pile smells, it's not getting enough air. Grass clippings are notorious for producing a foul odor when you put them in the compost heap green. If you insist on removing grass clippings from the lawn (they should be left on the lawn to decompose there), don't pile them all together in a heap where they will mat. Instead, mix or layer them with coarse materials through which some air can move. A brown layer of coarse dry stuff like brush, a wet layer of green stuff like grass or garden clippings, then a layer of soil is the recommended system of layering a compost heap, but anything close will move you in the direction of more efficient composting.

Remember: anything that was once living will eventually decompose. Why not let it decompose in the compost heap, where it can be of some use to you, instead of adding it to overloaded landfills? Many county and municipal governments have already started refusing to accept garden wastes in landfills. Why wait to be coerced into installing a gold mine in your backyard? Start your compost heap now.

December

Get Off the Dole— Plant Your Own Deodar Cedar

There comes a time in the life of every gardener when she knows her friends won't put up with her pilfering forever. Friends like Bernice Levin who has put up with my raiding her magnolia every Christmas for 24 years are the exception, but there usually comes a day when friends make it clear it's time to start growing your own greens. Having reached this stage with the owner of a particular deodar cedar about nine years ago, I finally planted my own, and it's an act of self-sufficiency I recommend for every self-respecting hall-decker.

What a joy it is to have my own deodar cedar, because this is one of the greens I enjoy working with most. This was the first year I allowed myself to cut more than a snippet or two of its branches, because I didn't want to stymie its growth, but now, after nine years of growing from its 2½-foot tall beginning, it is 20 feet tall and I feel free to cut. The feathery foliage of deodar cedar (*Cedrus deodara*) is a beautiful silvery green, and it has relatively soft, inch-long needles that spiral all the way around the branches. Because its branches have no front and back as so many evergreens do, they're a joy to use in arrangements. They are almost the opposite of American holly whose one-sided, dark, prickly leaves can arrange themselves into a big blob of black if you're not careful. Needles on graceful deodar cedar branches are also much less stiff than those of spruce or fir; it may be a bit of an overstatement to compare them to asparagus fern, but after one has spent a day arranging coarser greens, their delicate texture feels that fine.

The tree is beautiful in the landscape, too. As a young tree, deodar cedar is pyramid shaped, but with relatively loose, gracefully sweeping branches. When I was a child there was one in my backyard I loved so much that I swore to my mother that I was going to name my first child Deodora. My daughter Kate is glad I broke my promise, but I'm still drawn to deodar cedars wherever I see them. They are best located on large properties in full sun where they can be viewed from a distance and grow to their full size without engulfing a house. Probably the most beautiful deodar cedar in the country grows beside Custis Mansion at Arlington Cemetery; it's the biggest deodar cedar in Virginia at 70 feet tall with a 102-foot crown spread. A beautiful young deodar cedar grows in the front yard of the Hargrove's house on James Street in Ashland where we neighbors enjoy watching it get a new string of lights every year, but should it reach the size of the Arlington Cemetery tree, we'll have to build a bypass to get around it.

Unlike our native red cedar, which is really a juniper, *Cedrus deodara* is a *real* cedar like the Atlas cedar and Cedar-of-Lebanon. It's not a native tree; it was introduced to this country from the Himalayas in the 1830s. Of the many deodar cedar cultivars, plantsman Michael Dirr recommends 'Shalimar' because of its cold hardiness. Zone 7 is about as far north as you can plant this tree, and even there cold sometimes kills back the tops of the trees. That's the one problem with deodar cedars: quite often, just as they are growing to spectacular beauty, their tops die back. The problem can evidently be one of several things, or a combination of troubles. In his *Manual of Woody Landscape Plants*, Michael Dirr makes this notation about the cause of deodar cedar dieback: "canker (?), weevil, and/or cold."

Nurserymen recommend protecting deodar cedars from sweeping winds, and my experience suggests that's good advice. The first deodar cedar I planted about 15 years ago died on a windswept hill, but the one I'm cutting on now seems to be thriving on the leeward side of the same hill. Even there it's in a pretty exposed situation and often stressed by other factors, so I fully expect it to lose its leader, but I've come to expect older deodar cedars to have flat tops. Their sweeping branches remain unaffected, and they are no less useful as Christmas greens.

Unfortunately, that same windswept hill has claimed the lives of two other seedlings—both magnolias—that I planted in the interest of self-sufficiency. But have patience, Bernice, have patience; I've got a new seedling coming along.

Poet's Laurel Rides Up Front

If you take a close look at holiday arrangements from the florist, you will see one type of greenery that is used over and over again. It's Italian Ruscus, a tender evergreen with deep green, bamboo-like foliage that resembles the foliage of a related plant we can grow in our backyards—poet's laurel. Florists use Italian Ruscus the way amateur arrangers use poet's laurel, as a reliable evergreen filler. What's so great about poet's laurel is that its leaves (actually flattened stems) look as unblemished in December as they do in May, and they hold up an extraordinarily long time in arrangements. Even the plant's stems are green, and they have the stiffness of more woody-stemmed plants without their coarseness or heft.

This is a shrub that even postage-stamp gardens can accommodate, and it would make a great gift for a gardener who also loves flower arranging. To find it, you'll need to know its botanical name, *Danae racemosa*. Some nurserymen call it Alexandrian laurel and at least a few gardeners in Hanover call it porch laurel. "I must have heard porch laurel when someone said poet's laurel," says a friend. "The name seemed right because it grew at the end of the porch!"

Whatever you call it, this evergreen shrub is a treasure, but it's not a shrub you would pick out in the landscape for its handsomeness. Although it's tidy and elegant, with glossy foliage and occasional fat, red berries, it is usually small and inconspicuous, tucked away in a flower arranger's garden like a broach in a jewelry box. Only once have I seen poet's laurel make a significant statement in the landscape; that's at Westover plantation where a low, thick hedge of it beside a tenant's house looks almost like weeping bamboo. More often, it's a spindly 2- to 4-foot plant with gracefully arching branches that flop over other plants.

It is slow-growing, but that just makes arrangers covet it all the more. Some arrangers guard their poet's laurel more closely than they do their bank accounts, and if I see an arrangement into which an arranger has put several of her longest pieces of poet's laurel, I immediately think "big spender."

The best place to grow it is in a moist, well-drained spot with humus-rich soil and shade. Its leaves tend to burn when it gets too much sun, and I would say "don't plant this shrub in full sun" if it weren't for the plants at Westover, which seem to thrive there. That's a puzzle.

Poet's laurel has no serious disease or pest problems, but sometimes it does succumb to winter-kill. We in the Richmond area are near the limit of its cold hardiness range (zone 7), so it is wise to give your poet's laurel all the protection you can, such as planting it beside a building (think porch laurel) or near other shrubs that can block cold winds. Even under ideal conditions, don't expect it to reward you with rapid growth, however. Once established it grows faster, both from the tips and from new shoots that come up from the ground, but it's a notoriously slow starter. Nurseryman Butch Gaddy says the biggest poet's laurel he ever saw was a plant 4 feet tall and 6 feet wide (counting the spread of its weeping branches), and it was 30 years old.

Because I cut on mine, it's hard to know exactly how slow-growing it is, but it seems to be the slowest-growing shrub in the yard. Last year I divided my parent plant into four smaller ones hoping to increase production threefold; instead, I think I set them all back, because I saw almost no new growth all season.

A better way to get new plants is to watch for seedlings that sometimes pop up where the berries fall. They are not numerous, however, so if someone offers you a poet's laurel seedling, give it the respect it deserves. This fall, for example, I knew I had a knowledgeable gardener on my hands when, among other plants she'd come for, Rommy Harrington prepared to take home an 'Annabelle' hydrangea and a poet's laurel seedling I had given her. As she loaded her 'Annabelle' hydrangea into the bed of her truck, she apologized, "She'll have to lie down in the back." Then she opened the front door and prepared to place her more valuable poet's laurel. "He," she said knowingly, "gets to ride up in the cab."

Wild about Winterberry

When most of us think of hollies, we think of hollies with dark, shiny, evergreen leaves, but winterberry is a deciduous holly. Who would want a holly without its dark, shiny, evergreen leaves? Someone who loves red berries and dramatic landscape effects, that's who.

After it loses its leaves, winterberry becomes a mass of stiff gray stems lined with ¼-inch red berries—a spectacular sight in the woodland or garden. As its name suggests, winterberry is particularly dramatic in winter, and it's a show-stopper when snow is on the ground.

Winterberry is a native shrub but not a familiar one, possibly because of where it grows—in wet places. You will most often find it growing by streams and ponds or in low wooded areas, and I remember getting my feet soaking wet the day I tried to hop Ashland's Stony Run to get my first close-up look at winterberry. Those wet feet served me well, however, because when it came time to plant my own winterberry, I knew where to plant it—in a wet spot.

Near a building with no gutters where water tends to stand, I've planted river birches and winterberry, two native plants that enjoy moist conditions and each other's company. Both are thriving, not because of any special efforts on my part but because they like their new home.

Given plenty of water, winterberry will grow in full sun, but it's really happier in part shade. I have seen it used in roadside plantings in the proximity of ornamental grasses—a traffic-stopping combination. Where I enjoy this shrub most, however, is in a woodland setting where its red berries seem so unexpected. It's a great plant for a garden you want to make wildlife friendly because birds enjoy the berries. Grow plenty of it, however, because in addition to leaving some for the birds, you'll want to use some of these long wands of berries in winter arrangements where they provide instant height and drama. The shrub grows 6 to 10 feet tall and will reportedly spread equally wide, but I have never seen a winterberry that wasn't taller than it was wide, and the shrub has an upright habit, so it doesn't really take up that much "floor space" in the garden.

In addition to our native winterberry (*Ilex verticillata*), there are many winterberry cultivars that vary in growth habit, vigor, and berry color. 'Winter Red' and 'Carolina Cardinal' are two good ones, and they, like our native winterberry, don't require a male winterberry in the area to produce fruit; a nearby male American holly can pollinate them. The cultivar 'Sparkleberry,' on the other hand, requires a male with parentage similar to its own to produce berries, and the cultivar 'Apollo' is often recommended as its mate. I know a landscape consultant who, when he plants 'Sparkleberry,' puts two of these females in the same hole with one male 'Apollo.' Pretty kinky, but he says "Man, do I get fruit."

The only problem I've experienced with winterberry is chlorosis—a yellowing of the leaves. I was puzzled this summer when the foliage of a winterberry I'd planted on one side of a porch became chlorotic, while the foliage of a winterberry on the other side of the porch was a healthy dark green. I've heard it's a high pH that causes winterberry leaves to become chlorotic, the alkaline soil making iron unavailable to the plant. How I happen to have alkaline soil on one side of the porch and not on the other, I have no idea (did someone throw out wood ashes there?), but I'll have to correct it.

I could acidify the soil by adding sulfur or aluminum sulfate (a rate of 1½ pounds per 100 square feet is recommended for clay soil), but I dislike prescriptions, for fear of overdosing, I guess, and will probably just throw some acidic oak leaves on my winterberry and wait patiently for them to work their magic. If my winterberry's leaves are chlorotic again in the spring, Hanover master gardener Dr. Frank Boldridge tells me I should feed the plant with Miracle Grow which contains chelated iron, a soluble form of iron available to the plant even if the soil pH is too high.

It's hard to get pumped up about such problems right now, however, because even my winterberry that had the chlorotic leaves is loaded with berries. That's one of the nice things about winter landscape effects anyway—they attract attention without demanding maintenance. Pass by the red berries of your winterberry, admire them, then trot inside and flop down in front of the wood stove. Such are the pleasures of winter gardening.

Ivy Sleeps, Creeps, Leaps . . . and Drinks

"The first year it sleeps, the second year it creeps, the third year it leaps." Or so the popular wisdom regarding ivy goes. Although the yearly intervals may not be exact, the progression is surely right. The ivy I planted under my maple tree did nothing for what seemed like ages, then started running across the ground, then grew 15 feet up the tree overnight.

I was thrilled. There's something venerable about ivy that appeals to me, but I know there are other people who associate it with disrepair, abandoned buildings, and neglect. Some also berate it for invading natural areas and wresting territory from native plants. The latter is a legitimate concern, but ivy's reputation for destroying brickwork and killing trees is probably overblown. Where mortar is defective or bricks cracked, ivy will exacerbate the problem, but I have seen a 35-year-old wall of ivy pull away from a 40-year-old wall of brick, leaving the wall perfectly intact. There's also good evidence ivy doesn't harm healthy trees. It's a climbing vine, not a parasite, and its roots don't penetrate bark unless the bark has already been violated. "Ivy doesn't really hurt a tree as long as it doesn't hide the foliage and reduce photosynthesis," says Richmond arborist Joel Koci.

I love the way ivy looks draped over shrubs and climbing up trees, and if it makes the garden look a little untidy, so much the better. "A little studied negligence is becoming to a garden," writes Eleanor Perenyi in *Green Thoughts*. "It blurs the edges— always supposing there are edges to blur. Painters love gardens on the fringe of neglect." How reassuring!

My neighbor Sarah Wright cautions me that the weight of ivy will pull over a rotten old tree, but I've also seen old snag trees beloved by woodpeckers that wouldn't be standing if ivy weren't holding them up.

Fact is, the only way to have the most beautiful ivy is to let it grow up and grow old. English ivy (*Hedera helix*) has two distinct stages. In its juvenile stage, it has the wonderful three- to five-lobed leaves we're so familiar with. But if it's allowed to grow up (to a height of at least 10 feet) and to attain a certain age (about 15 years), it takes on a different form. The lobes of its leaves get less pointed and more smooth-edged, its stems thicken, and it puts out short branches that are almost shrub-like. These "arborescent" vines produce tiny yellow-green flow-ers and clusters of blue-black berries. "That's the kind of ivy I want," I remember telling my husband once when we saw a Williamsburg wall covered with beautiful fruiting ivy. Little did I know it was the kind I already had, just older.

Some of the most beautiful old ivy in Ashland grows on the old cedars in a nearby cemetery. It's full of berries, and where the berries have either fallen off or been eaten by the birds, you can see a tiny bright magenta patch where the berry was at-tached to the stem. It's like getting to see a little puddle of the pure color that's always just suggested beneath the surface of an ivy leaf stem.

Ivy growing up on a picket fence also has a singular charac-ter. If the fence is about waist or chest high, the ivy will climb to the top then flop over forming a graceful curve in its stem. If you pull this ivy back to a little below where it is attached to the fence, you will get an ivy vine with closely spaced leaves, no aerial roots, and a natural curve that makes it easy to trail from bouquets and floral arrangements or to tie to banisters and use as Christmas garlands.

It's a great vine to grow for wildlife, too. Where ivy has been allowed to grow up and become dense, it provides cover and nesting sites for birds. Birds also eat its berries. Ivy flowers attract butterflies and a great buzzing of other insects, and I'm told ivy flowers are particularly valuable to honeybees, because unlike some flowers, their fall flowers yield nectar at all temper-atures and under nearly all conditions. The berries are poison-ous to us.

There are dozens of varieties of English ivy with varying growth habits and with varying physical features like variegated leaves, but not all of them are reliably hardy in Virginia. For that reason, the best place to get a new ivy is from a neighbor in whose yard it has proven hardy. One of my favorite ivies was given to me by Sarah Wright. It has a light green ruffled leaf, and Sarah calls it Japanese fan ivy. In my yard it has just begun to creep along the edge of a low border edged with stones. Sarah says it won't climb, although it's been circling a redbud in her yard as if it intended to climb it for years. Another ivy I treasure was given to me by my sister. It's a tiny little ivy with glossy, dark green, half-inch leaves with slightly wavy margins, *H. helix* 'Ivalace,' I think. My sister, who doesn't trust my reassurances about ivy and brickwork, has trouble keeping it from growing up the side of her brick house, so lustily does it grow, but mine is still sleeping. When I need really good ivy for arrangements, I go to my sister's and help her pull this gorgeous stuff off her house.

Ivy will grow most anywhere, even under greedy trees like Norway maples. You can start it from rooted runners or take cuttings which root easily in water. The only "ivy hassle" is keeping it in bounds, but there always seems to be one day each summer when the ground is too dry to do anything else and cutting back the ivy seems the thing to do. And there is nothing like a towering pile of ivy trimmings to make you think you've done a good day's work. For those who hate ivy trimming, and some do because thick ivy makes them think snakes, I've read that researchers are developing growth regulators that could be sprayed on ivy to keep it in check. I've also run the lawn mower over an overgrown bed of ivy and had it come back just fine, only tidier.

Ivy roots are incredibly opportunistic. I know my ivy is always just a clip away from outrunning me, but so far I've been able to catch it before it muscled its way out of my reach on our frame house or insinuated itself too far under the floorboards of the porch. Not so lucky were the caretakers at Magdalen College, Oxford who, so the story goes, noticed the ivy on the college wall was looking particularly happy but didn't know why until they discovered its runners had got into the cellar and drunk a whole barrel of port.

On Landscaping with a Chain Saw

"The axe is my pencil," wrote a Dutch landscape designer. Wrote another landscaper, "for all good effects of foliage in landscape gardening—after the fifth year—the axe is quite as important an implement as the spade."

I'm pondering these pronouncements because I'm just back from taking down trees. Notice the phrasing. It makes felling trees sound as easy, and as prosaic, as taking down curtains. What I'm wondering is if I have really just returned from slaying trees. At this moment I would do it again, and, in fact, I'm planning to. Last week my husband and I "took down" six 28-year-old loblolly pines on our Buckingham property; as soon as possible, we'll take down six more. We're doing it to improve a view.

About eight years ago we started this project. We felled a dozen or so 60-foot loblolly pines on the crest of our hill overlooking the James River where they were blocking our view of a beautiful pasture on the other side of the river. As those trees came down, I remember watching in awe as a new vista emerged; it was like watching an artist unroll a canvas. For the trees, I felt little or nothing. They were just loblolly pines, fast-growing trees of which we had plenty, and even if we didn't, every pine plantation in the state did.

But before we had finished taking all the pines down, houses started going up on the other side of the river and the wisdom of further opening up the view came into question. We decided we had better wait before taking any more trees down. As the years passed, the threat of more houses diminished, the trees grew. "Why don't you take those trees down?" nearly everyone who visited asked, because the trees sat in the middle of the horizon like a gigantic man blocking one's view of a movie screen.

Last weekend, when we finally got around to tackling the

job, my first impression was of how much the trees had grown. What might have been a big job eight years ago was going to be a herculean task now. The trees were about 70 feet tall, the largest 20 inches in diameter, the smallest about 12 inches. I could go on about the experience of taking them down: how smart I was to figure out which one should go first, how terrified I was every time John revved up the chain saw (women whose husbands spend a lot of time riding tractors and using chain saws should get the same sympathy policemen's wives do). But the experiences that really impressed me that day had more to do with the trees than us.

First I was impressed with what a difference the trees' removal made in the ground-level experience of the landscape. Yes, there was no question that the view from the house was better without the trees, but I was going to miss the anchoring presence of these big trunks among the smaller cedars that surrounded them. We had also opened up big chunks in the canopy which, by letting light in, would encourage invasive plants like the honeysuckle. I'd have to keep an eye on that.

A second impression was more confusing. I was standing at the very top of one of the pines now lying on the ground. My job was to carry off the brush, but John was still working his way up the trunk, cutting off logs, so I was absentmindedly pulling cones off the top branches. As I was wresting a cone free, my fingers were surrounding a twig about a half inch in diameter when John leaned into the trunk with his chain saw. He was about 25 feet away, pressing the saw into thick wood; I was barely touching a twig near the top of the tree, but I felt every vibration—every rev, every pause, every deep-throated run—of the chain saw. It was as if an electric current had passed through the tree to me.

I don't want to get too mushy about this; I know these were just vibrations traveling though wood, but the experience startled and moved me. At the very least, it impressed on me the fact that what we were doing was being felt in ways that I had been formerly unaware of. Felt: that's an interesting word choice, too. That trees are sentient beings, I know intellectually. But I have felt it in the way a mother feels a baby's pulse only once, maybe twice. The time I'm sure I felt it came after a day of reading about lenticels—the breathing holes in the bark of trees. You can see them in cherry trees: they are like little slits in the bark. I went out to see them one winter day and "felt" a cherry tree breathe. Not physically exactly; the tree's "breath" didn't stir the hairs on my face, but some "sense of life" passed between us. I've never felt quite the same thing since.

To understand my experience taking trees down now, you must also know that should I die and come back as a tree, I would think I had moved up. I think this business about higher forms of life is all a big conceit and that any life form that does its business without speech is a higher form. Who is really to say which is the top, which the bottom, of the evolutionary ladder; didn't Einstein say time moves both ways? So I don't take the removal of a tree lightly. On the other hand, I am not of the "all life is sacred" school. Nature is pretty flip about life. So are gardeners; we pull out a thousand seedlings a day with nary a protest from a single right-to-lifer. Why my view of a river should have precedence over the life of a tree, I don't know. Maybe I'm not highly evolved enough to see otherwise yet. Maybe feeling that chain saw vibration was like a quickening — the beginning of a better sense of what it means to be a tree and of my relationship to trees. I don't know.

A last impression of that tree-felling is worth relating. On the stump of the trees we'd cut down, John and I counted 28 rings. To be truthful, on some we counted only 27, but it is likely the trees were all planted the same year and we decided to go with 28 because the day before, December 28, was our twenty-eighth wedding anniversary. I suppose I could go off on the cosmic implications of this, but what is really significant about the coincidence is that it gave me such an undeniable benchmark by which to measure the life of the tree. It had stood as long as I had been married, might have been planted the day I stood before a Justice of the Peace in Dillon, South Carolina, with my love beside me. Yes, tree, I know what 28 years means.

Our local forester Bill Ruby says loblolly pines mature at 50, start to break up around 80. If I were a better poet or tree-lover, I'd insist we leave two pines standing on the hillside, just to watch them grow. But right now I'm into landscaping, which is too bad for six fine trees.

Afterword

I would much prefer to have ended a book about my gardening experiences with an essay about planting a tree. But my reflections in the final essay about cutting trees down are closest to where my thoughts about gardening are heading, so it seemed appropriate to include them in a final chapter. It's not that I'm becoming ax-happy. Far from it; the older I get, the more appreciative I become of anything that took a long time to get where it is. And in terms of making a meaningful mark on the landscape, any gardening activity less significant than planting a tree begins to seem like busywork. But my last essay seems to express the paradox in gardening— the inherent contradiction in changing nature to make things look more natural, in destroying some plants to celebrate others, and in imposing our visions of beauty on a landscape that was "right" before us and will be "right" after us. What I understand only poorly but trust the garden to teach me is how my vision of beauty itself is part of the process, no less natural than a bee or a bud. The only thing I know for sure is that as my sympathetic understanding of plants increases, my vision of what is worth doing, and truly beautiful, improves. It's on the strength of that knowledge that I continue gardening, and it is with confidence in that outcome that I recommend the experience.

A Note on References

The books I consult most often for gardening information include the following:

Encyclopedia of Gardening, written primarily by James Crockett and published by Time-Life between 1971 and 1978

Wyman's Gardening Encyclopedia by Donald Wyman, published by Macmillan in 1971

Manual of Woody Landscape Plants by Michael A. Dirr, published by Stipes Publishing Co. in 1990

The Wildlife Gardener by John V. Dennis, published by Alfred A. Knopf in 1985

Growing and Propagating Wild Flowers by Harry R. Phillips, published by the University of North Carolina Press in 1985

Tree Maintenance by P. P. Pirone et al., published by Oxford University Press in 1988

Saving Seeds: The Gardener's Guide to Growing and Storing Vegetables and Flower Seeds by Marc Rogers, published by Storey Communications, Inc., in 1990

Seed Germination Theory and Practice, published by Norman C. Deno in 1993